THE WISDOM TREE SERIES

Quotes of J. KRISHNAMURTI

Compiled by Harish Dhillon

AUSTRALIA • CANADA • HONG KONG • INDIA
SOUTH AFRICA • UNITED KINGDOM • UNITED STATES

Hay House Publishers (India) Pvt. Ltd.
Muskaan Complex, Plot No.3, B-2 Vasant Kunj, New Delhi-110 070, India
Hay House Inc., PO Box 5100, Carlsbad, CA 92018-5100, USA
Hay House UK, Ltd., 292-B Kensal Rd., London W10 5BE, UK
Hay House Australia Pty Ltd., 18/36 Ralph St., Alexandria NSW 2015, Australia
Hay House SA (Pty) Ltd., PO Box 990, Witkoppen 2068, South Africa
Hay House Publishing, Ltd., 17/F, One Hysan Ave., Causeway Bay, Hong Kong
Raincoast, 9050 Shaughnessy St., Vancouver, BC V6P 6E5, Canada

Email: contact@hayhouse.co.in
www.hayhouse.co.in

Designed by Aeshna Roy at Hay House India

ISBN 9789380480794

Printed and bound at
Replika Press Pvt. Ltd.

Introduction

Jiddu Krishnamurti, or J. Krishnamurti was born on 12 May 1895 in Andhra Pradesh, the eighth of eleven children, in a Telugu-speaking Brahmin family. His father, an official in the British colonial administration, retired in 1907 and found employment as a clerk in the headquarters of the Theosophical Society at Adyar (Chennai).

While an adolescent, Jiddu had a chance encounter with C. W. Leadbeater, a high ranking theosophist. Leadbeater was also a well known occultist with a reputation of being something of a clairvoyant. He noticed at once the wonderful aura that emanated from Krishnamurti, in which there was not a particle of selfishness. He predicted great things for the lad and recommended him to Annie

Besant, the leading light of the Theosophical Society.

She was as impressed as Leadbeater had been and the two took the young Krishnamurti under their tutelage, convinced that he was destined to be a great world teacher. As a result, Krishnamurthi and his brother Nitya, were privately tutored and then sent abroad for higher education.

The daily programme followed during this period of private tuition included rigorous training in sports, the pursuit of academic subjects, theosophical and religious lessons, yoga and meditation and lessons in the ways of British Society and culture.

Krishnamurti showed a natural inclination and ability for sports but no particular interest in academics. He showed a flair for languages and was comfortable speaking in many foreign tongues. He also enjoyed studying the Bible and Western classics. He showed great observation and mechanical skills and even in childhood could correctly disassemble and reassemble fairly complicated machinery.

The Theosophical leadership then established a new organization called the 'Order of the Star in the East.' The purpose of this was to prepare the world for Krishnamurti's emergence as a world teacher and Krishnamurti himself was appointed the head of the Order.

Obviously at this stage Krishnamurti subscribed to and approved of his future role as a world teacher. In his capacity as the head of this new Order, Krishnamurti went around the world giving lectures and conducting meetings and discussions.

During one of these travels to America, Krishnamurti was enchanted by the Ojai Valley in California. Thus his supporters bought a cottage and the surrounding land, which was to become not only Krishnamurti's official residence, but also his 'home'.

In August 1922, Krishnamurti went through what he was to call a 'life changing experience'. Till this time, his spiritual progress had followed the path prescribed by the leaders of the Theosophical Society. Now he took the first step to becoming an individual and evolving along his own unique path.

In the years that followed, Krishnamurti's new vision and conviction continued to develop till in 1929, he disavowed his role as a world teacher and dissolved the order.

Krishnamurti now denounced all organized belief, the notion of gurus and the whole teacher-follower relationship and worked to set man free. He claimed allegiance to no nationality, caste, religion or philosophy. He spent the rest of his life travelling around the world as an individual speaker. Maintaining that society is ultimately the product of the interactions of individuals, he held that fundamental societal change can emerge only through freely undertaken radical change in the individual.

He constantly stressed the need for a revolution in the psyche of every human being and emphasized that such revolution cannot be brought about by any external entity; be it religious, political, or social.

He authored a number of books, among them *The First, Last Freedom, The Only Revolution* and *Krishnamurti's Notebook*. A large number of his collected talks and discussions have also been published.

He was awarded the 1984 United Nations Peace Medal and two years later addressed the United Nations on peace and awareness.

He died in Ojai on February 17, 1986 at the age of 90. His remains were cremated and scattered by friends and former associates in the three countries where he had spent most of his life: India, England and the United States.

Krishnamurti's writings and the compilations of his speeches and discussions remain as popular today as they were when they were first published. Supporters, working through several non-profit foundations, oversee a number of independent schools centered on his views on education in India, the UK and the United States, and continue to transcribe and distribute many of his thousands of talks, discussions, and other writings.

The core of all Krishnamurti's teachings is best summed up in a statement he made in 1929:

'Truth is a pathless land. Man cannot come to it through any organization, through any creed, through any dogma, priest or ritual, nor through any philosophical knowledge or psychological technique. He has to find it through the mirror of relationship through the understanding of the contents of his own mind through observation, and not through intellectual analysis or introspective dissection. Man has built in himself images as a sense of security – religious, political, personal. These manifest as symbols, ideas, beliefs. The burden of these dominates man's thinking, relationships and his daily life. These are the causes of our problem for they divide man from man in every relationship.'

– Harish Dhillon

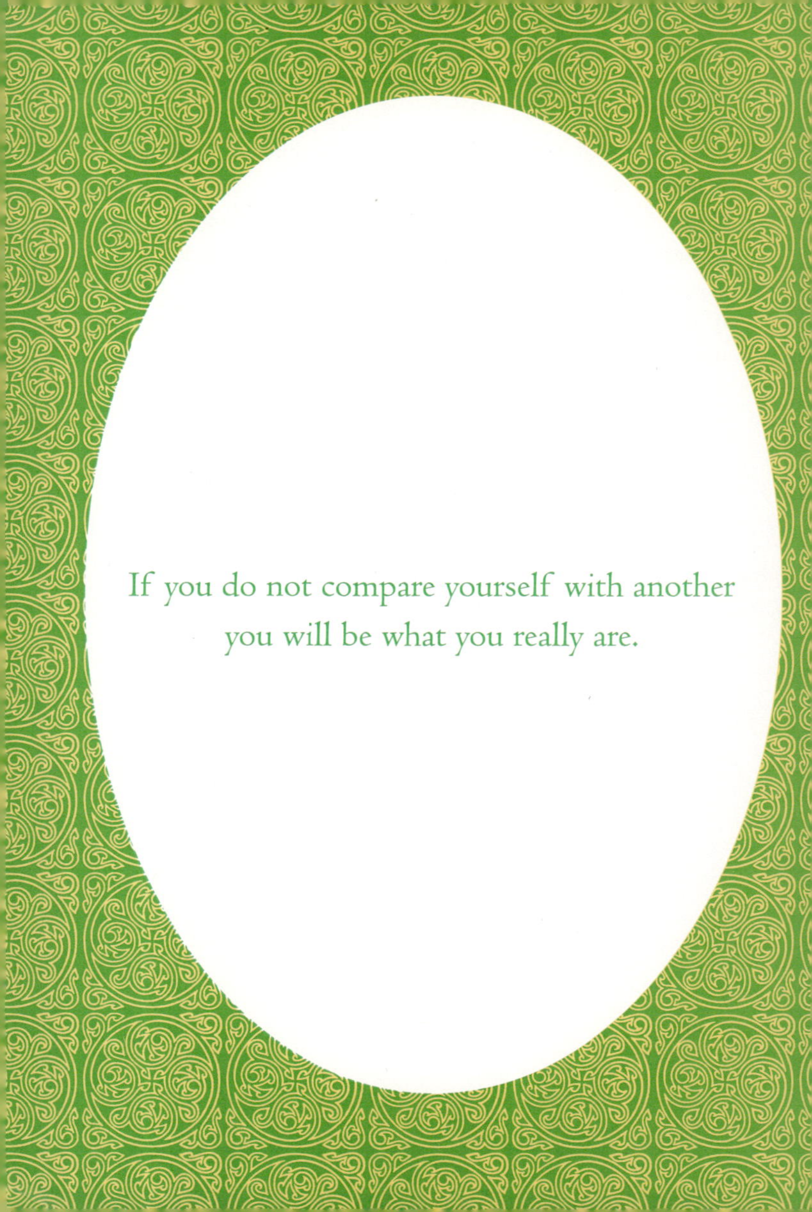

If you do not compare yourself with another
you will be what you really are.

A mind that is all the time seeking pleasure must inevitably find its shadow in pain.

Freedom is a state of mind –
not freedom from something.

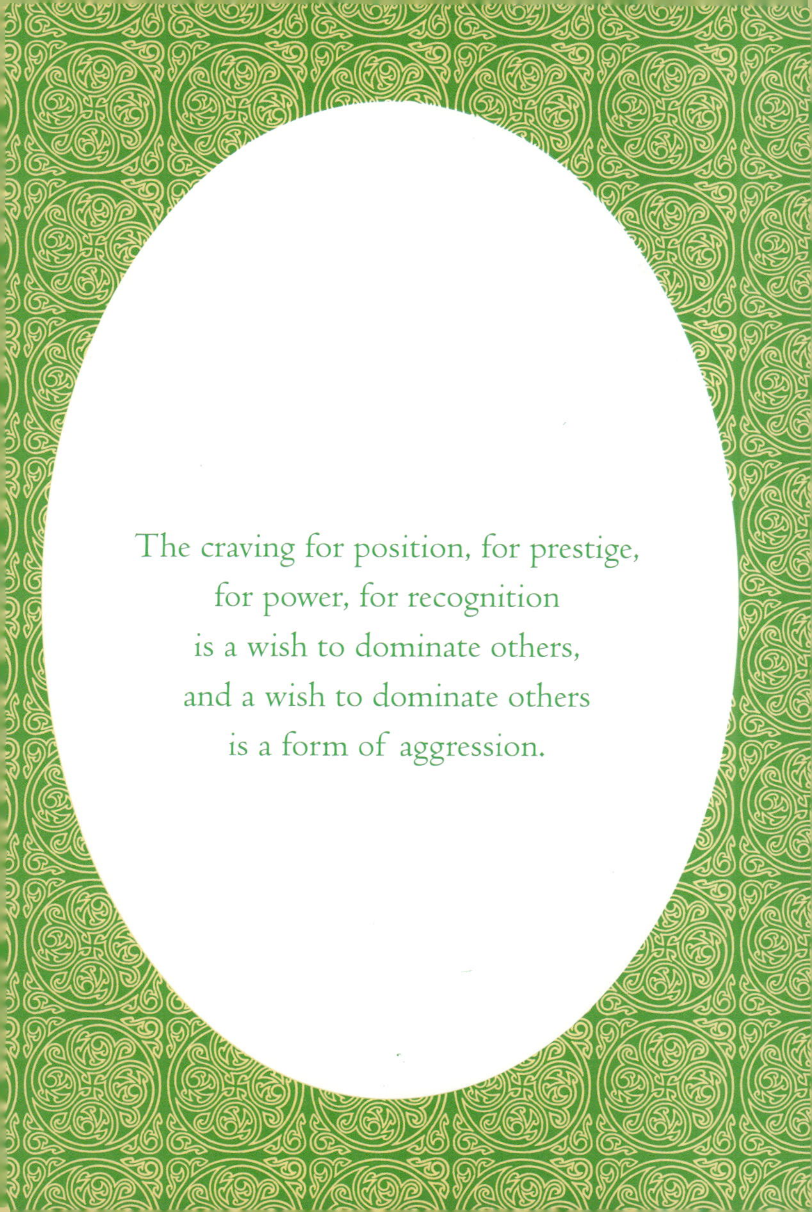

The craving for position, for prestige,
for power, for recognition
is a wish to dominate others,
and a wish to dominate others
is a form of aggression.

A mind that is caught in fear
lives in confinement, in conflict
and therefore is violent,
distorted, and aggressive.

To understand yourself
is the beginning of wisdom.

If one allows a problem to endure,
it distorts the mind.

To have inward solitude and space
implies freedom to be, to go, to fly.

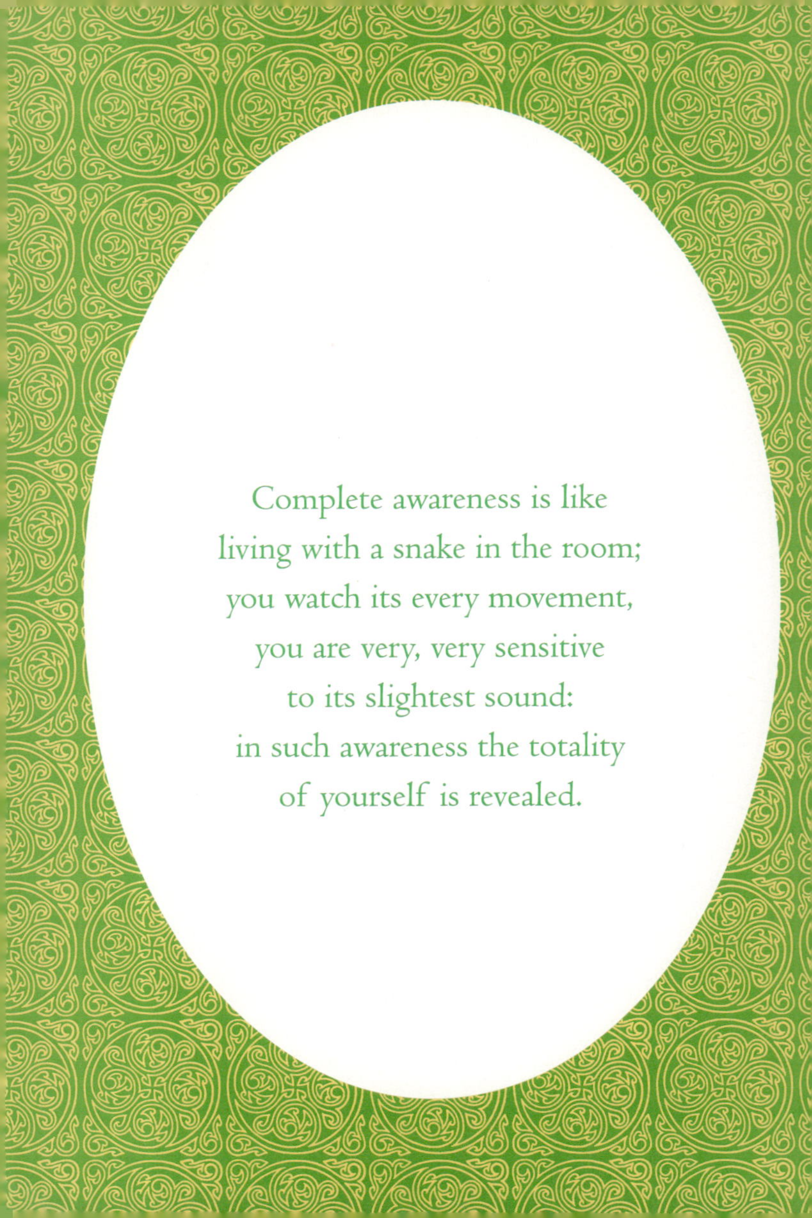

Complete awareness is like
living with a snake in the room;
you watch its every movement,
you are very, very sensitive
to its slightest sound:
in such awareness the totality
of yourself is revealed.

To live completely, fully, in the moment
is to live with what is, the actual,
without any sense of
condemnation or justification.

To be alone you must die to the past.

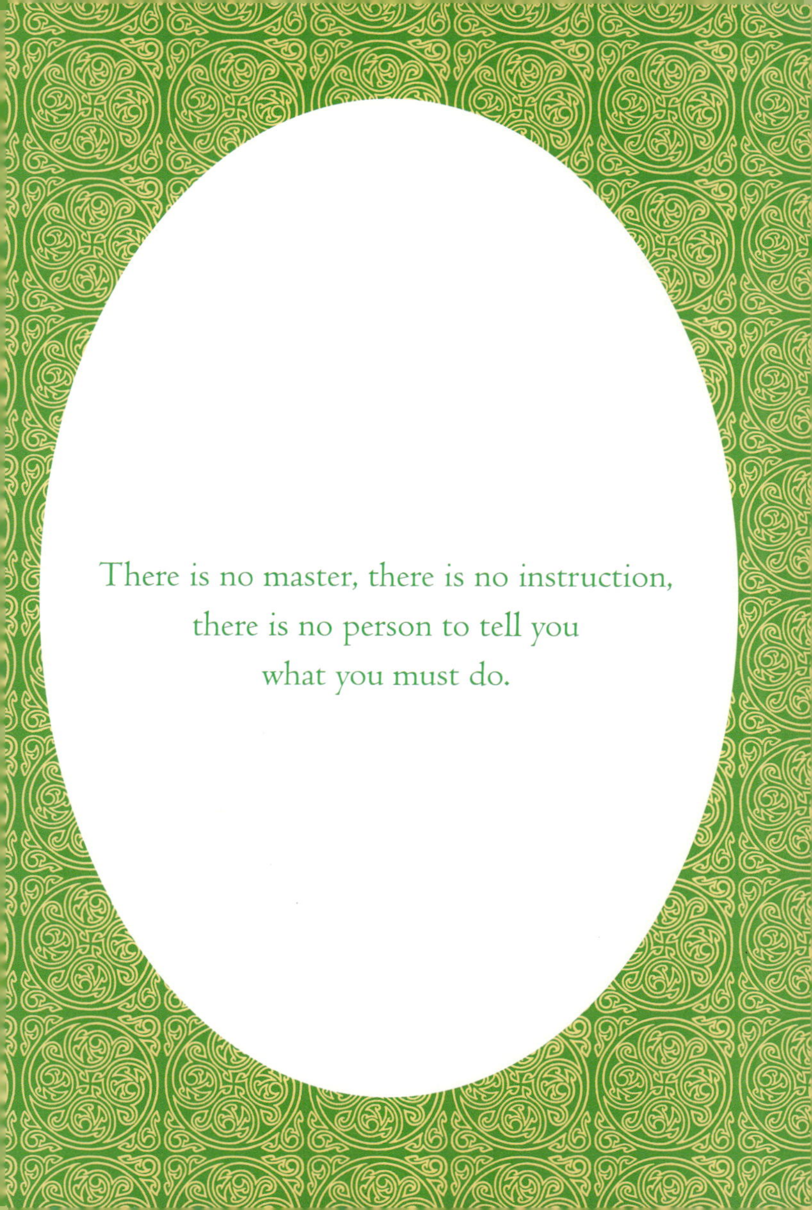

There is no master, there is no instruction,
there is no person to tell you
what you must do.

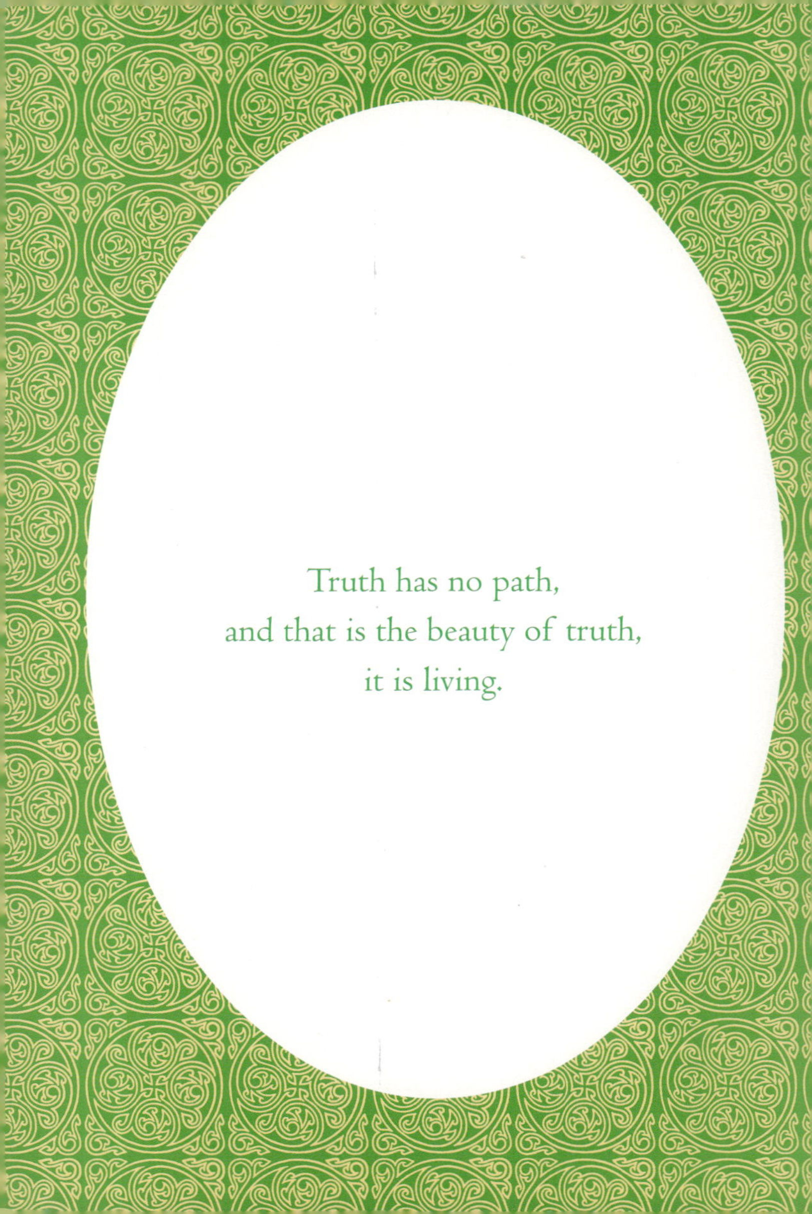

Truth has no path,
and that is the beauty of truth,
it is living.

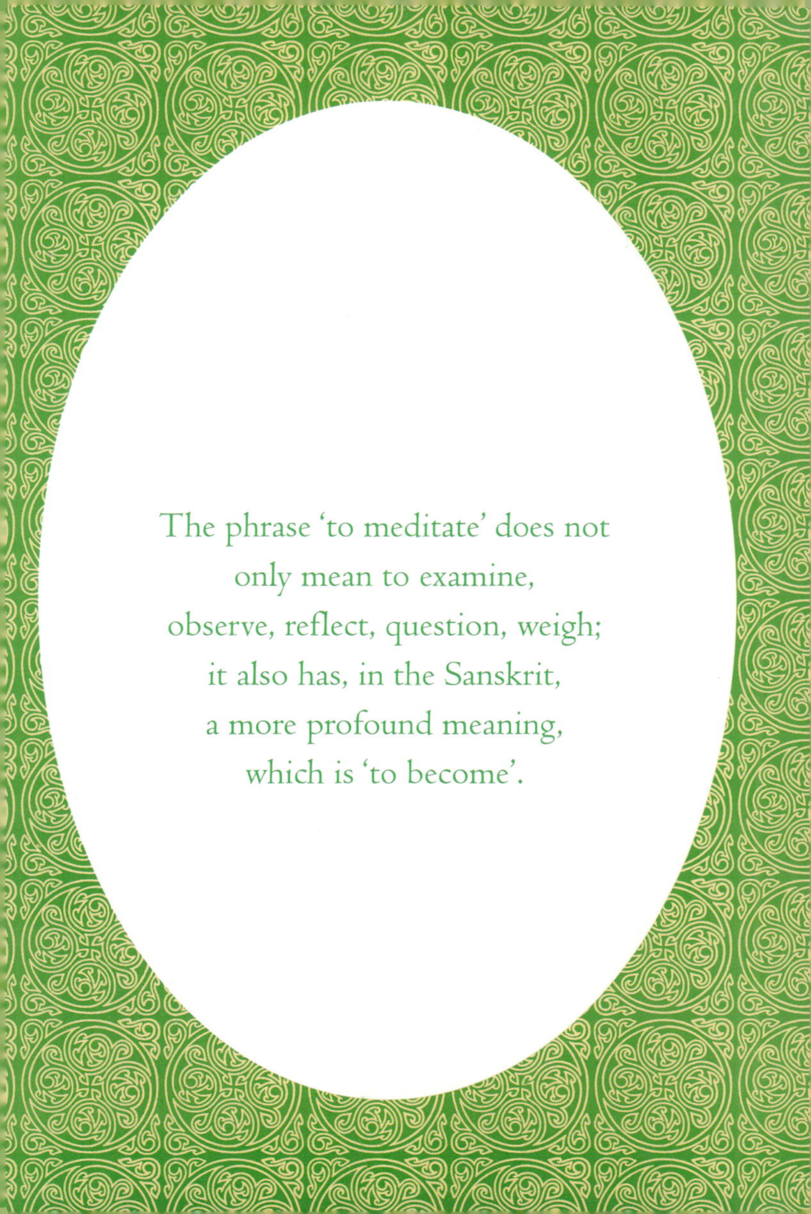

The phrase 'to meditate' does not
only mean to examine,
observe, reflect, question, weigh;
it also has, in the Sanskrit,
a more profound meaning,
which is 'to become'.

Never under any circumstances say 'how'.
When you use the word 'how'
you really want someone to tell you what to do,
some guide, some system, someone to lead you
by the hand so that you loose your freedom.

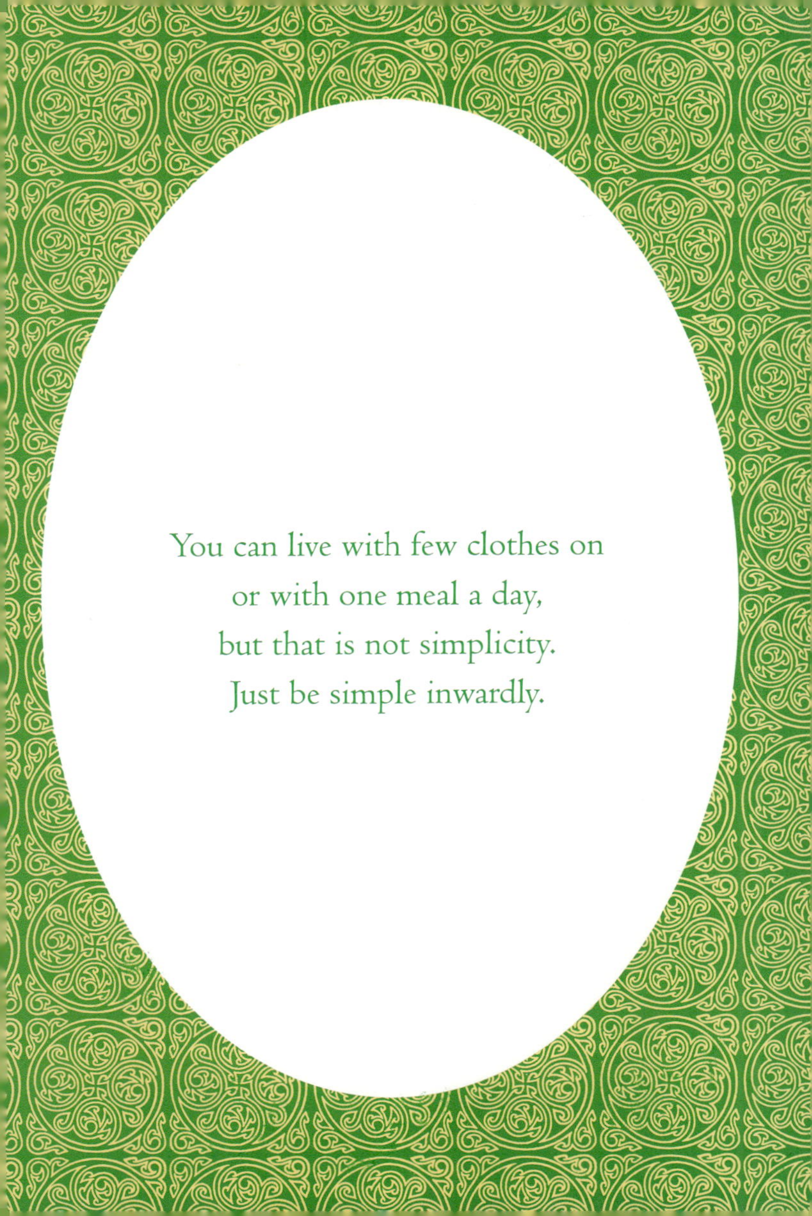

You can live with few clothes on
or with one meal a day,
but that is not simplicity.
Just be simple inwardly.

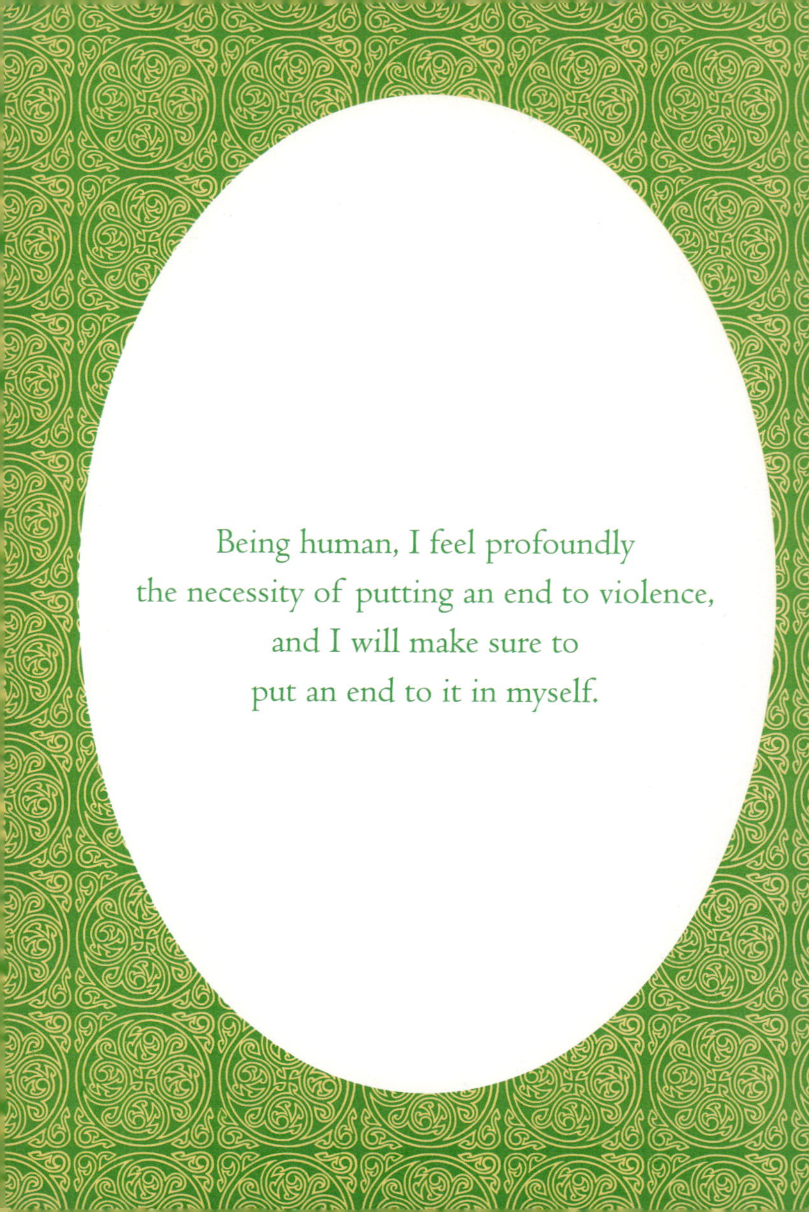

Being human, I feel profoundly
the necessity of putting an end to violence,
and I will make sure to
put an end to it in myself.

A mind that is burdened with the past
is a sorrowful mind.

Violence is not merely killing another.
It is violence when we use a sharp word,
when we make a gesture to brush away a person,
when we obey because there is fear.

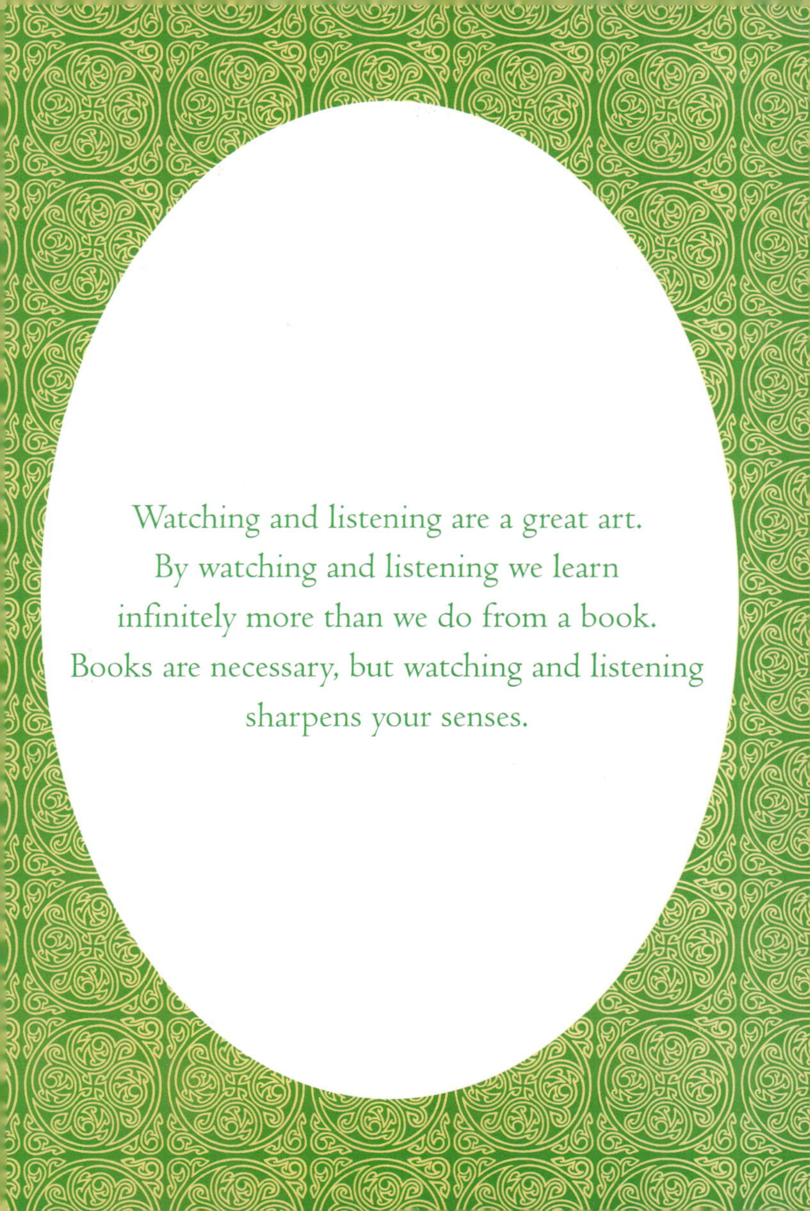

Watching and listening are a great art.
By watching and listening we learn
infinitely more than we do from a book.
Books are necessary, but watching and listening
sharpens your senses.

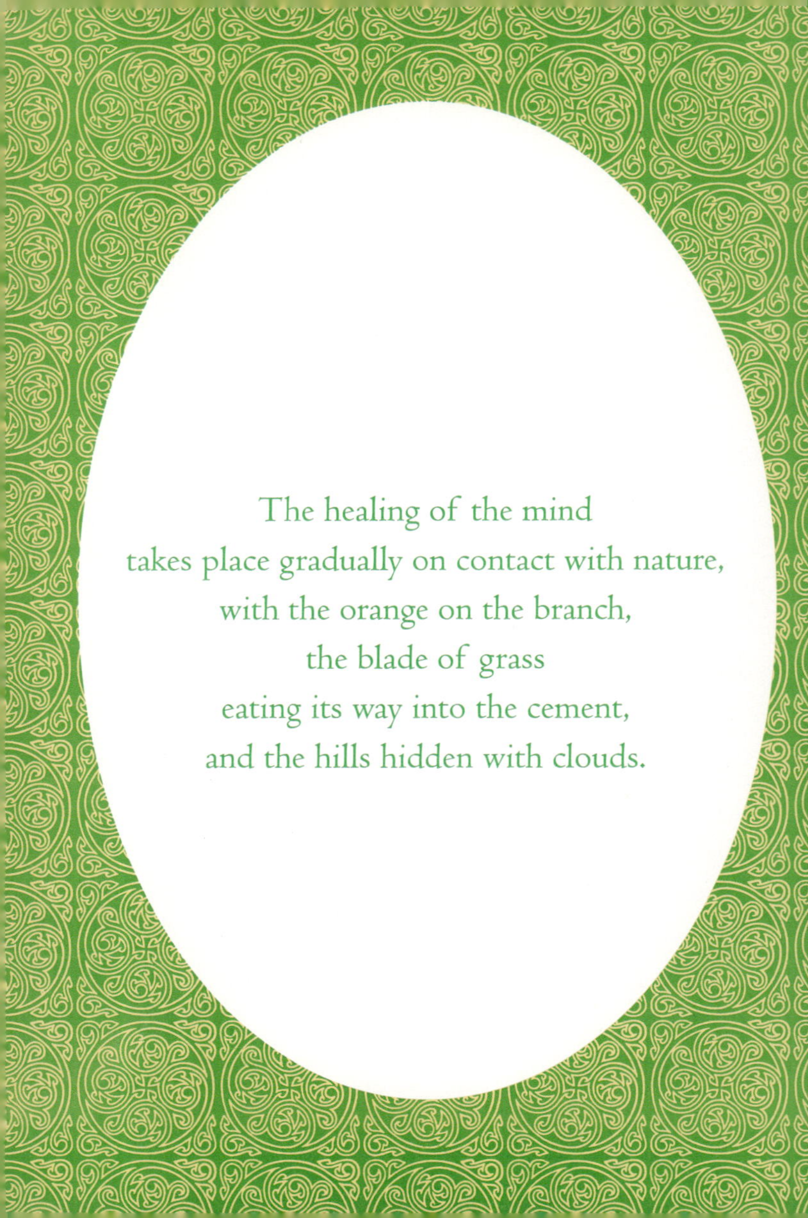

The healing of the mind
takes place gradually on contact with nature,
with the orange on the branch,
the blade of grass
eating its way into the cement,
and the hills hidden with clouds.

My country and your country,
my God and your God –
all that is the fragmentation of thought.

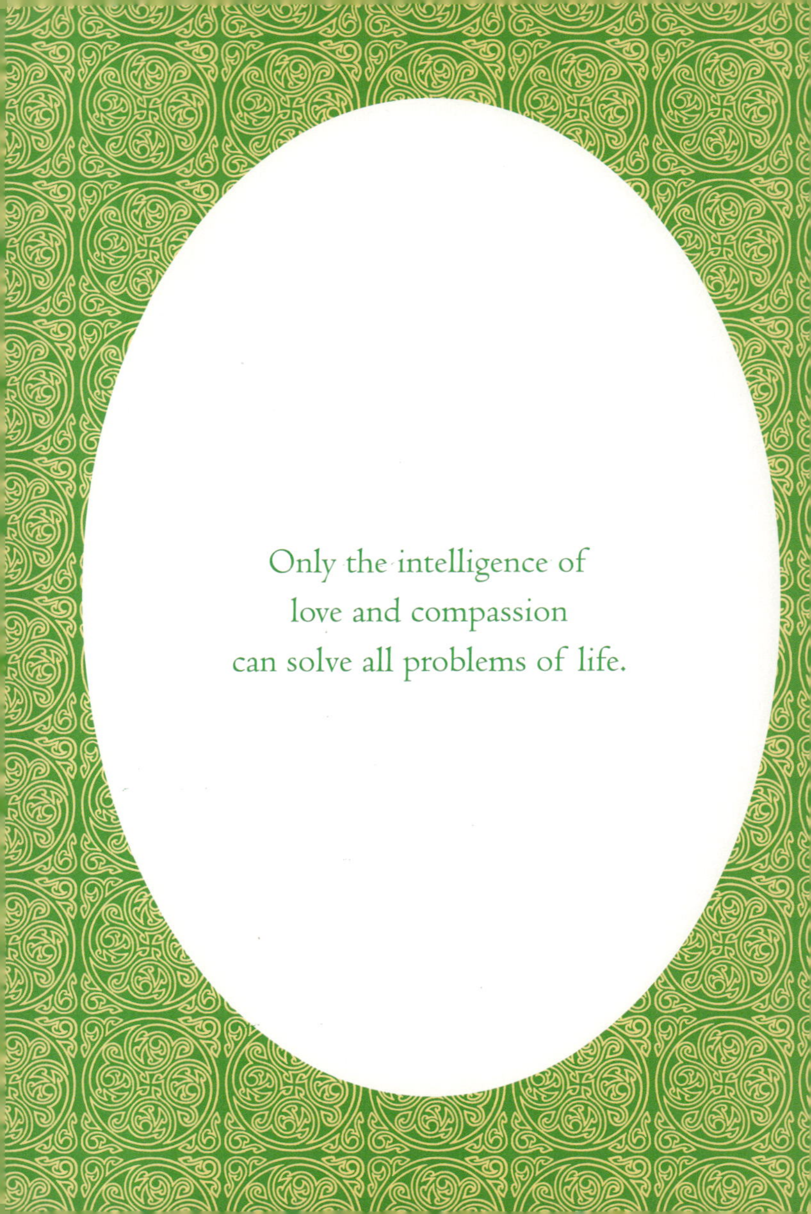

Only the intelligence of
love and compassion
can solve all problems of life.

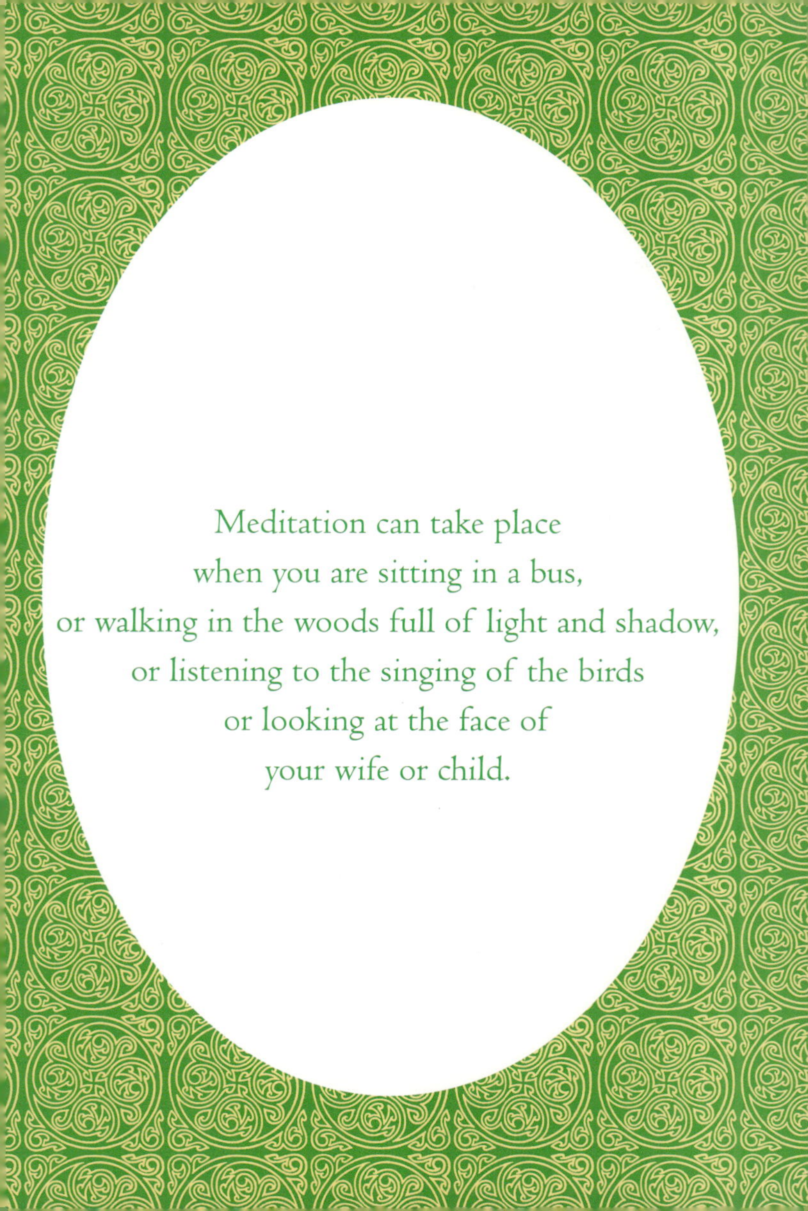

Meditation can take place
when you are sitting in a bus,
or walking in the woods full of light and shadow,
or listening to the singing of the birds
or looking at the face of
your wife or child.

Love can come into being only when there is total self-abandonment.

Society cannot change unless man changes.

When you separate yourself by belief,
by nationality, by tradition,
it breeds violence.

Facts are not frightening.
But if you try to avoid them,
turn your back on them and run,
then it is frightening.

Propaganda can never tell the truth,
truth can never be propagated.

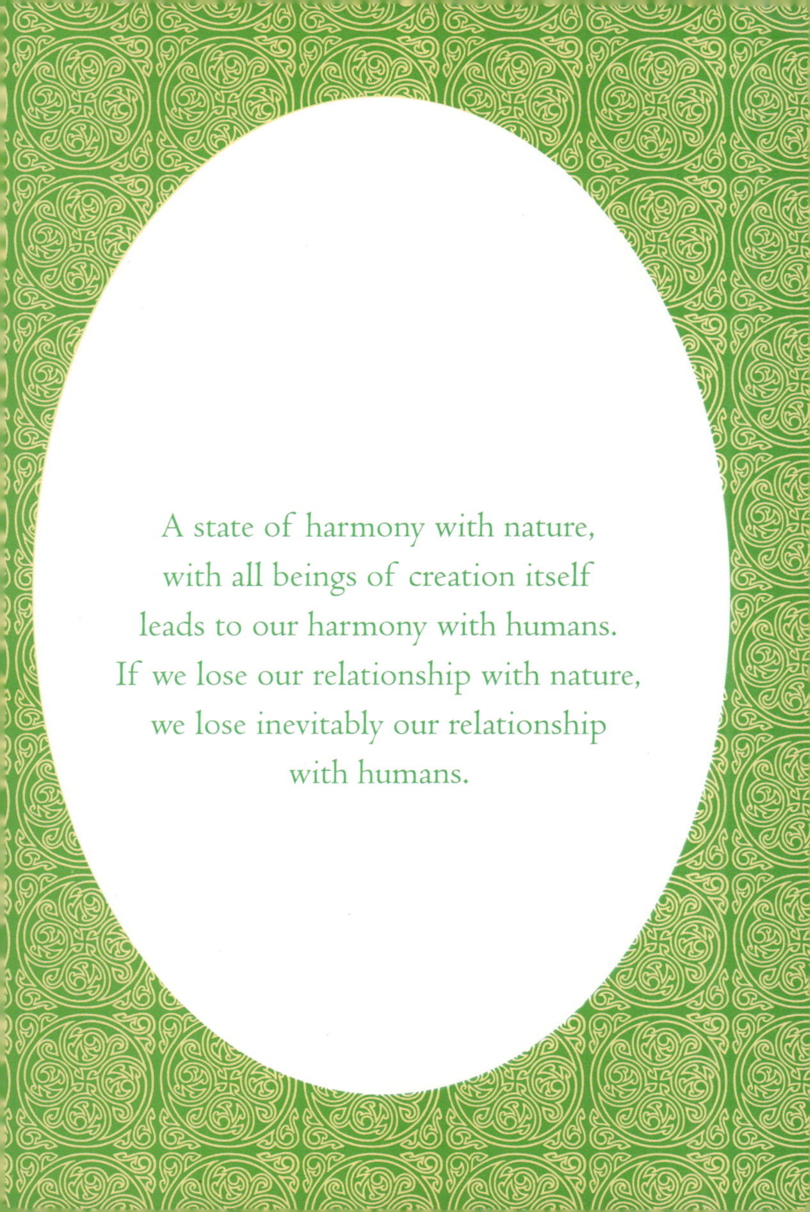

A state of harmony with nature,
with all beings of creation itself
leads to our harmony with humans.
If we lose our relationship with nature,
we lose inevitably our relationship
with humans.

Truth is that which one wishes in its totality.

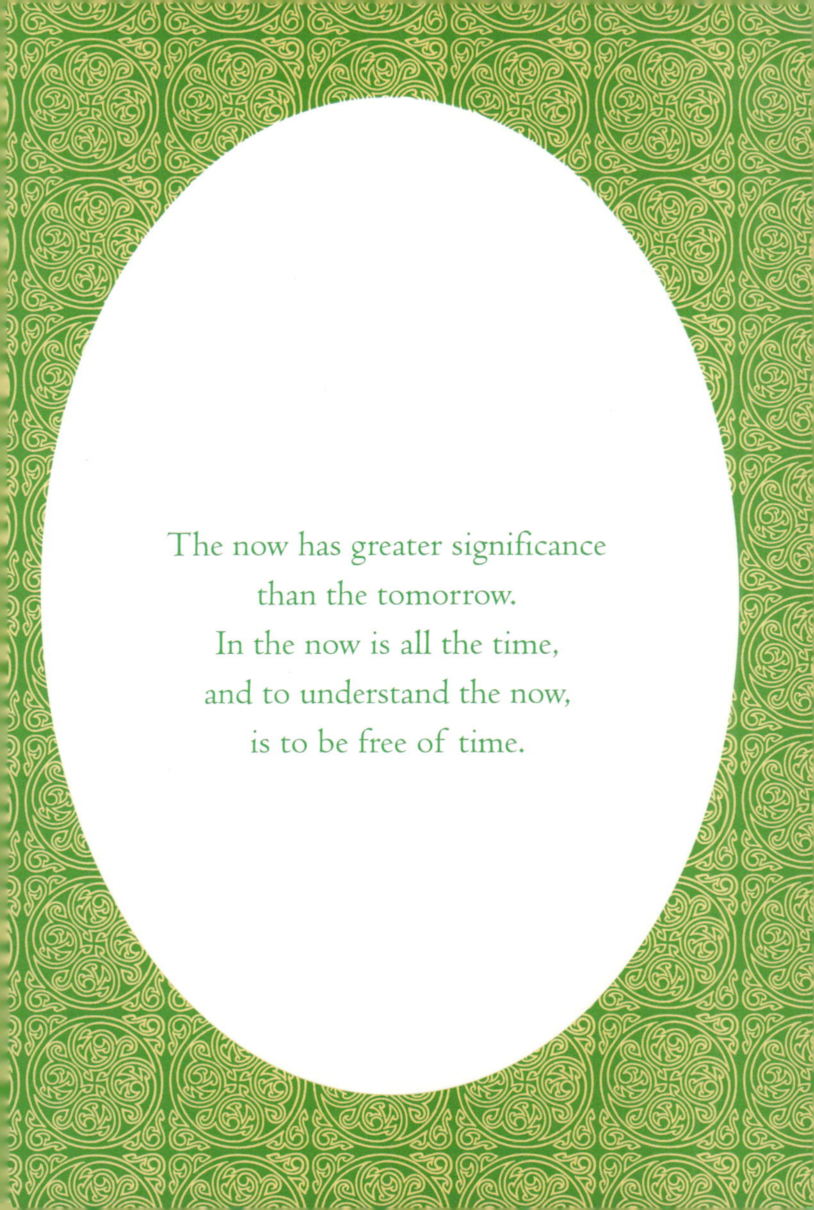

The now has greater significance
than the tomorrow.
In the now is all the time,
and to understand the now,
is to be free of time.

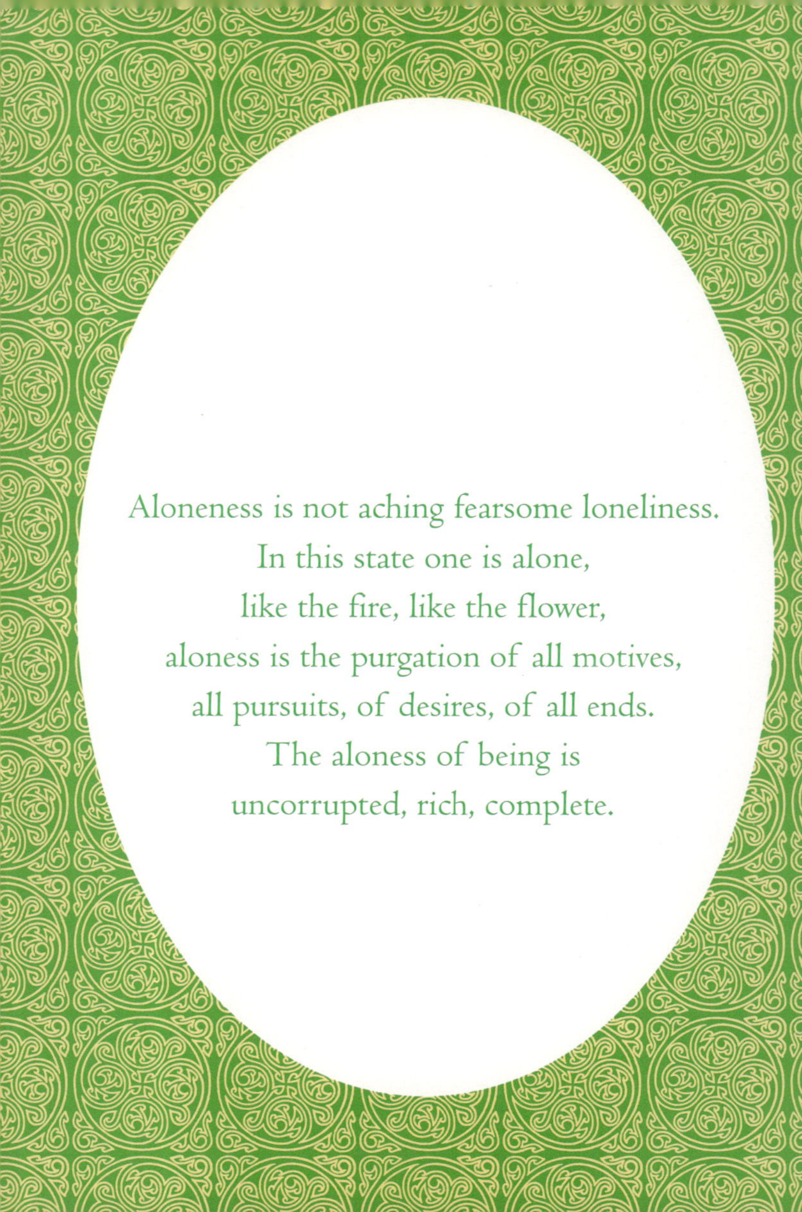

Aloneness is not aching fearsome loneliness.
In this state one is alone,
like the fire, like the flower,
aloneness is the purgation of all motives,
all pursuits, of desires, of all ends.
The aloneness of being is
uncorrupted, rich, complete.

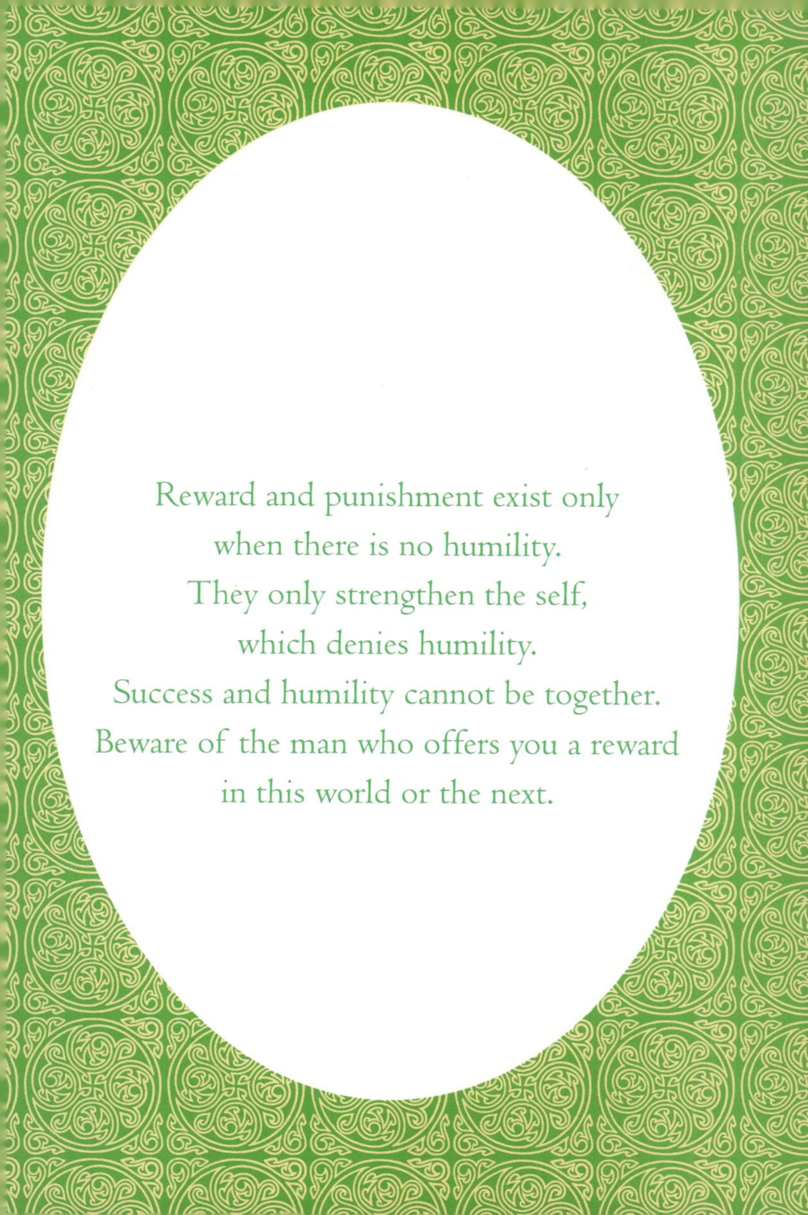

Reward and punishment exist only
when there is no humility.
They only strengthen the self,
which denies humility.
Success and humility cannot be together.
Beware of the man who offers you a reward
in this world or the next.

With so much poverty
and degradation all around,
one must have a very thick skin to be rich.

A mind burdened with becoming
can never be tranquil.

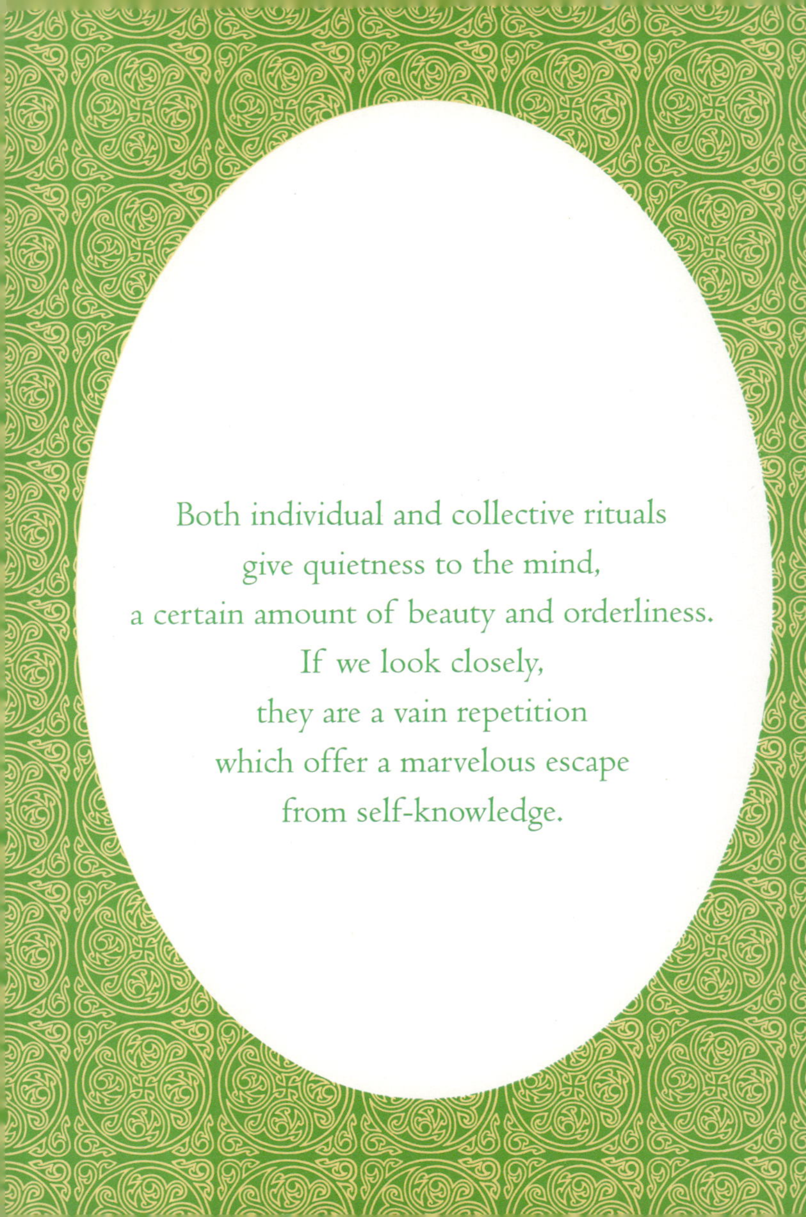

Both individual and collective rituals
give quietness to the mind,
a certain amount of beauty and orderliness.
If we look closely,
they are a vain repetition
which offer a marvelous escape
from self-knowledge.

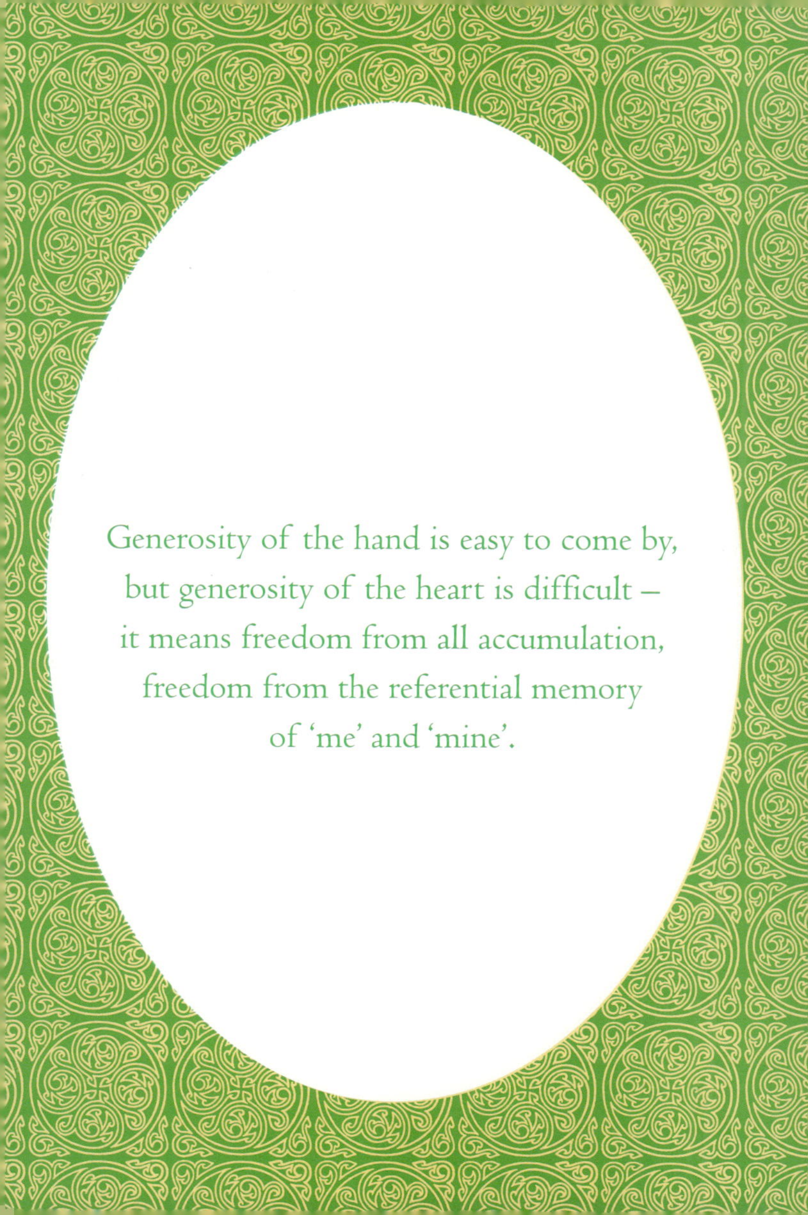

Generosity of the hand is easy to come by,
but generosity of the heart is difficult –
it means freedom from all accumulation,
freedom from the referential memory
of 'me' and 'mine'.

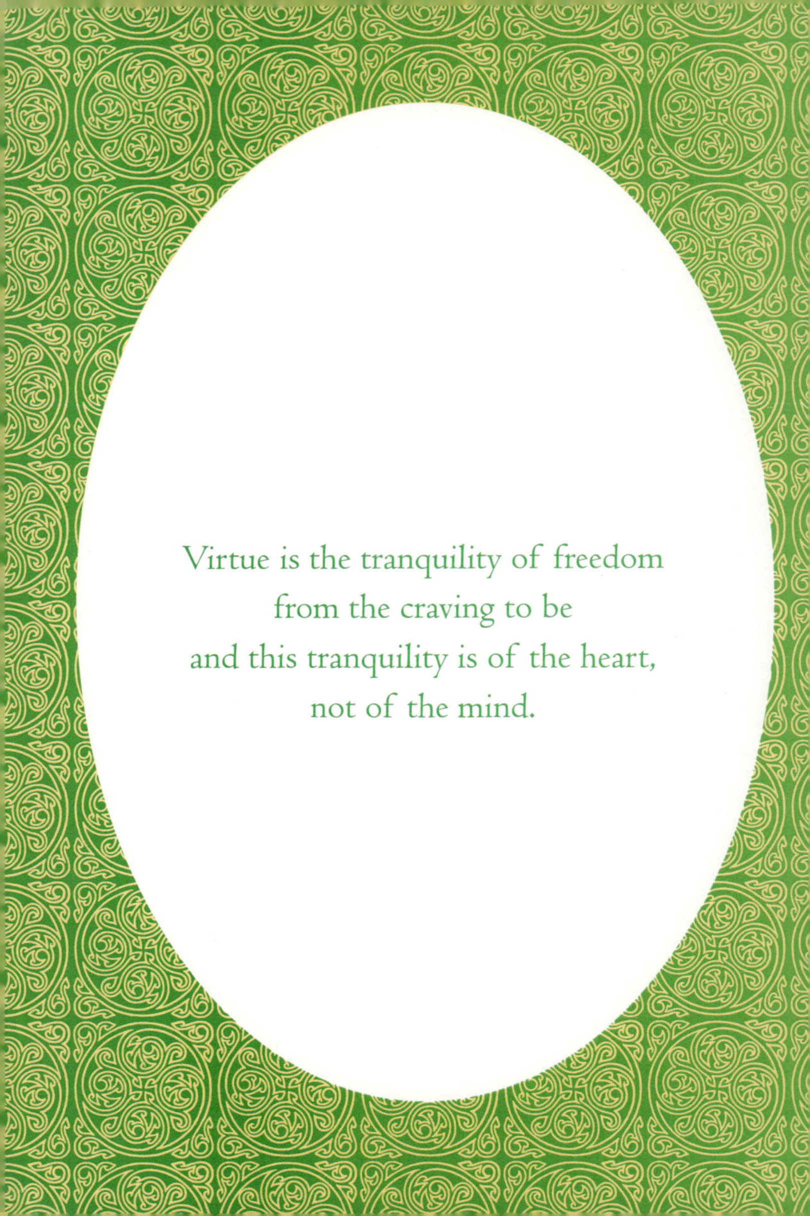

Virtue is the tranquility of freedom
from the craving to be
and this tranquility is of the heart,
not of the mind.

Right meditation is essential
for the purgation of the mind,
for without the emptying of the mind
there can be no renewal.

Mere continuity is decay.
The mind withers away by constant repetition,
by sensations which make it dull and weary.

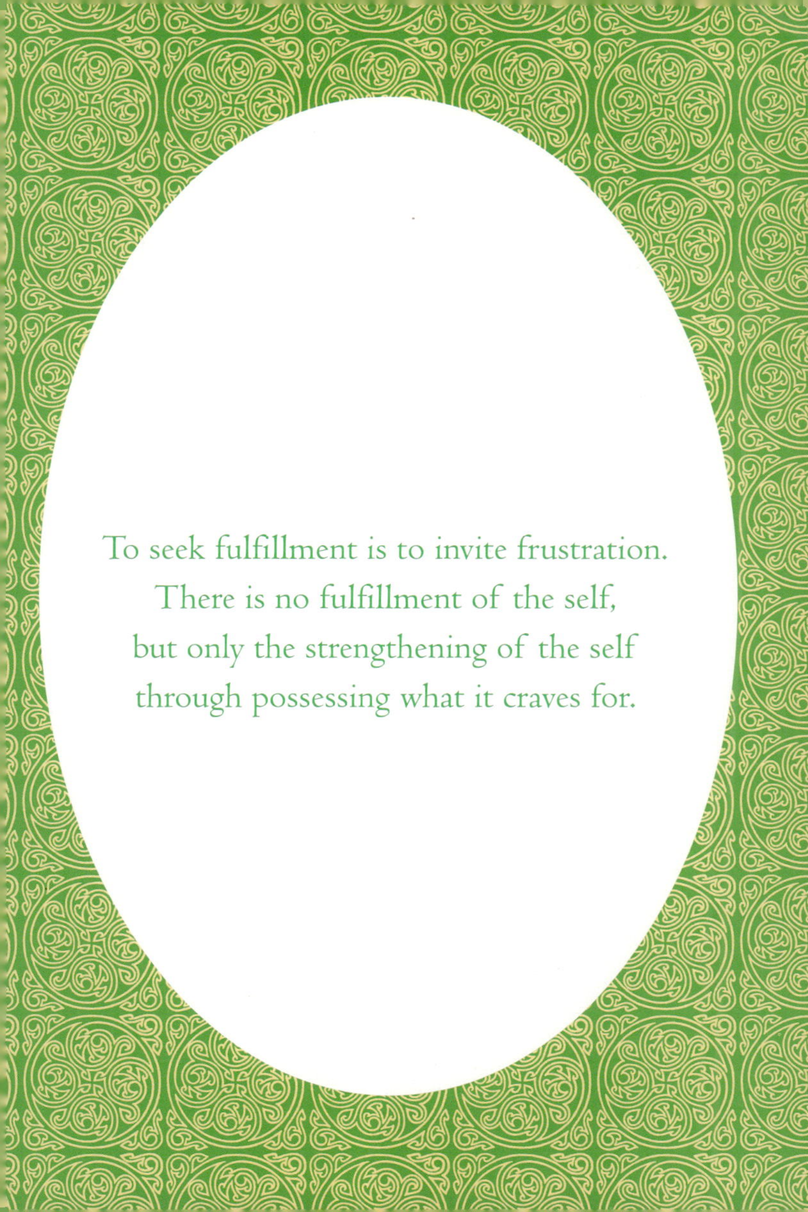

To seek fulfillment is to invite frustration.
There is no fulfillment of the self,
but only the strengthening of the self
through possessing what it craves for.

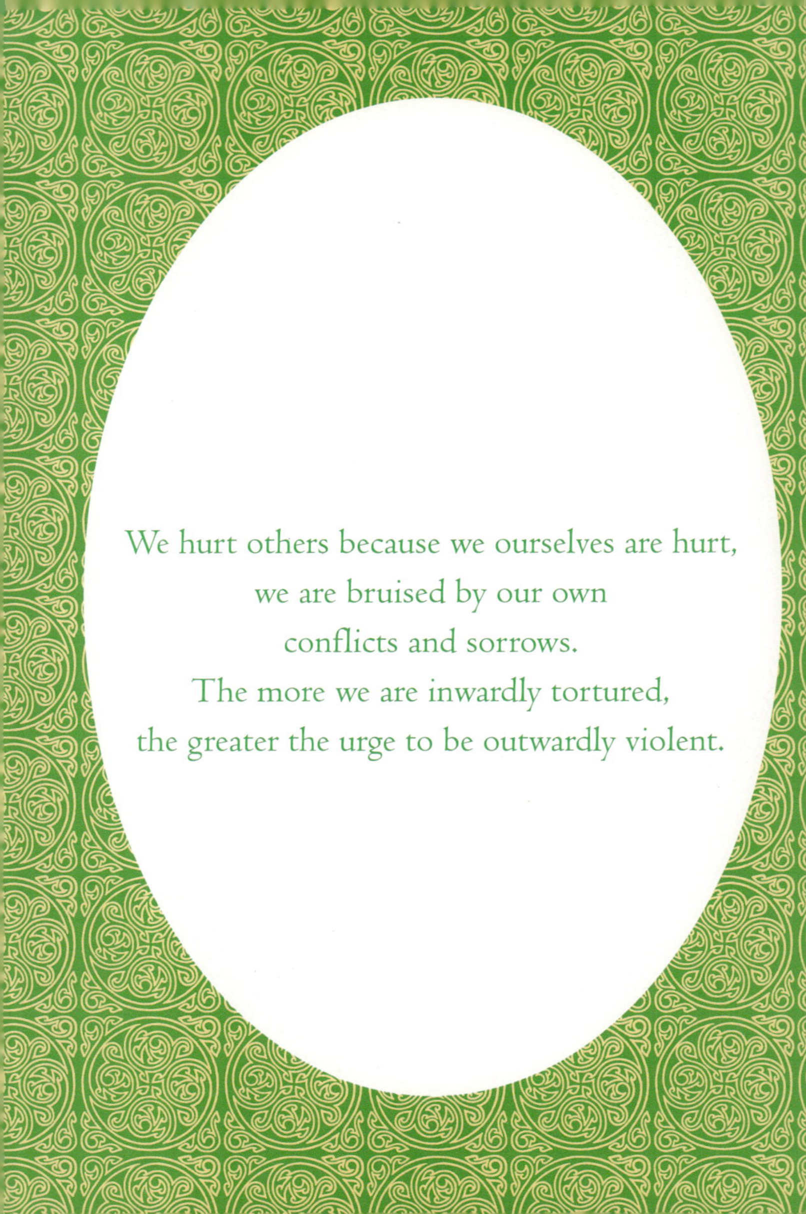

We hurt others because we ourselves are hurt,
we are bruised by our own
conflicts and sorrows.
The more we are inwardly tortured,
the greater the urge to be outwardly violent.

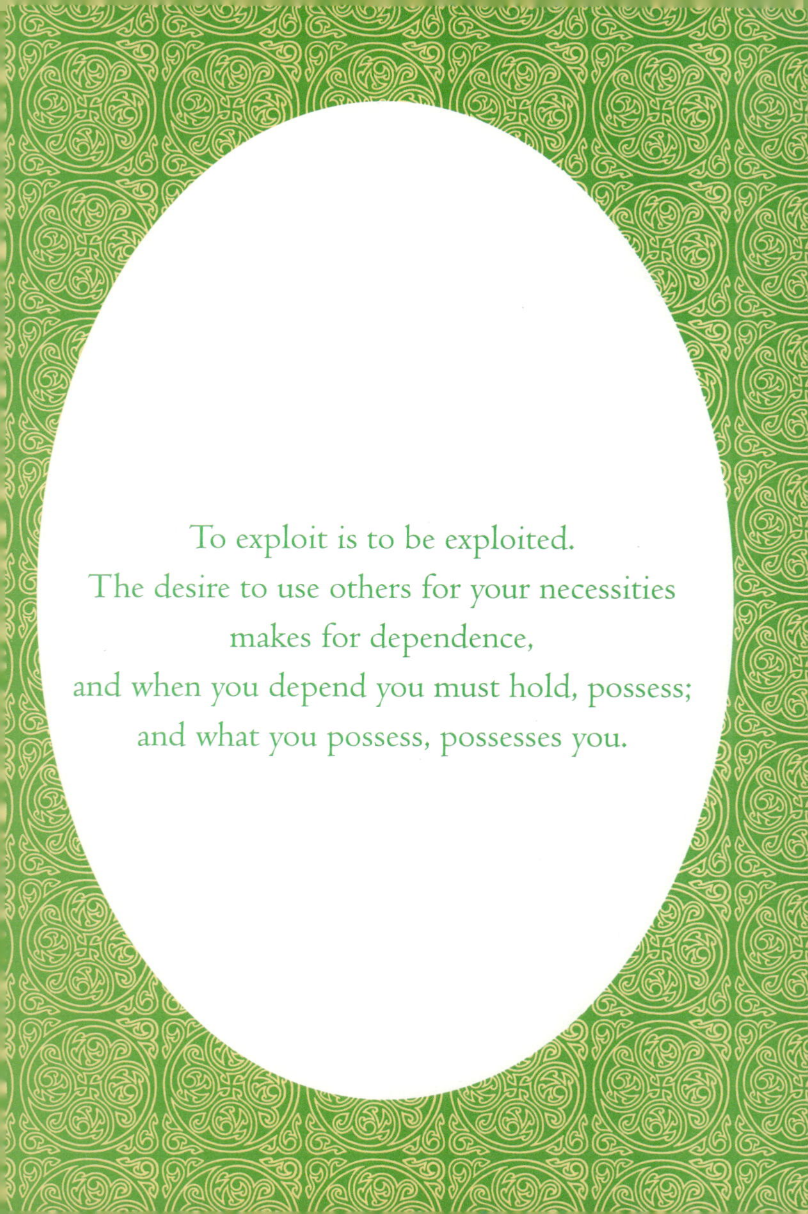

To exploit is to be exploited.
The desire to use others for your necessities
makes for dependence,
and when you depend you must hold, possess;
and what you possess, possesses you.

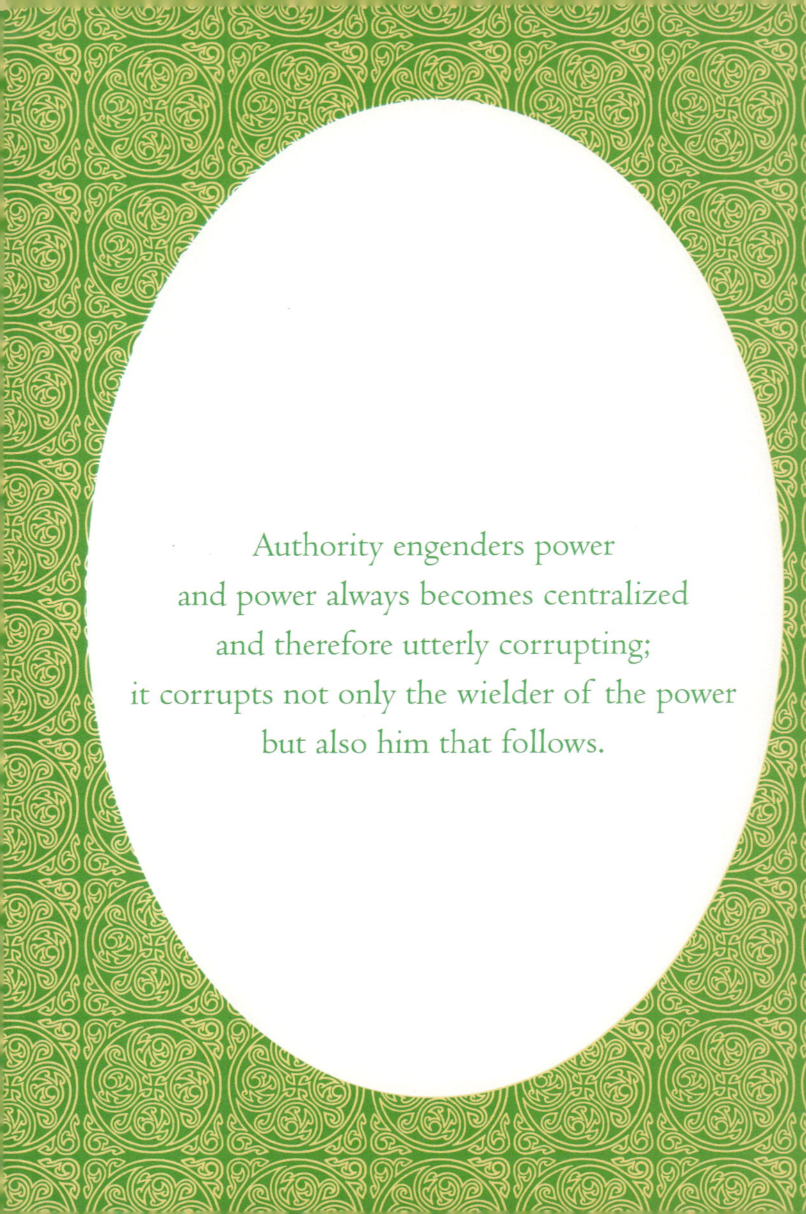
Authority engenders power
and power always becomes centralized
and therefore utterly corrupting;
it corrupts not only the wielder of the power
but also him that follows.

Happiness through something
must invariably beget conflict,
for then the means is vastly more significant
and important than happiness itself.

To search for what is beyond the actual
is to be caught in illusion.

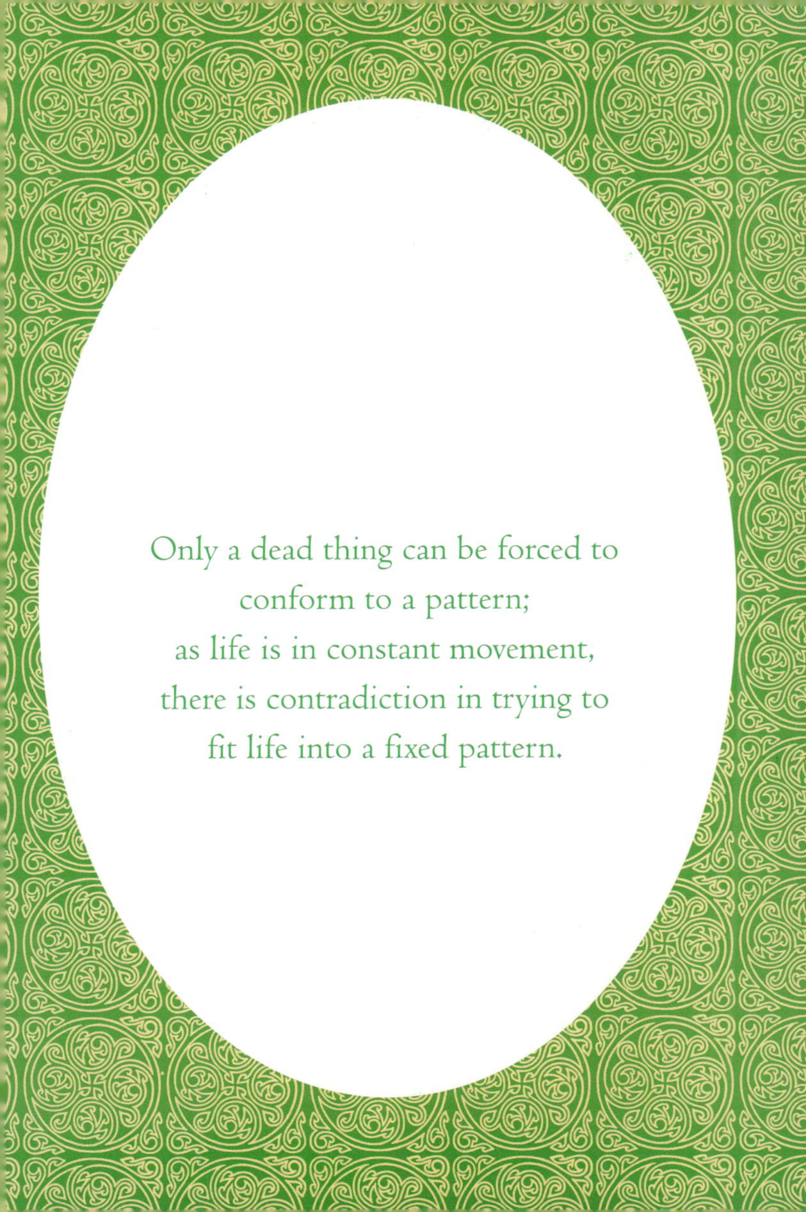

Only a dead thing can be forced to
conform to a pattern;
as life is in constant movement,
there is contradiction in trying to
fit life into a fixed pattern.

Where there is light, darkness is not;
darkness cannot conceal light.
Where jealousy is, love is not;
jealousy cannot cover love.

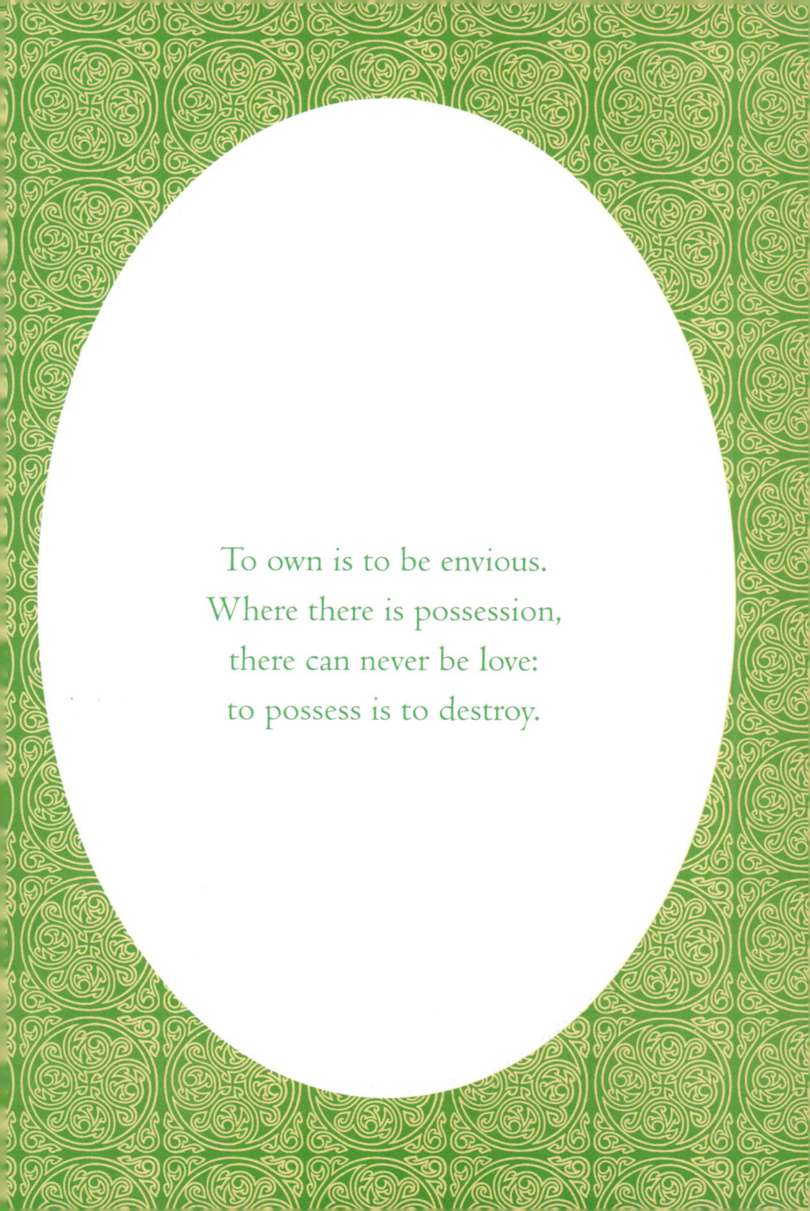

To own is to be envious.
Where there is possession,
there can never be love:
to possess is to destroy.

Truth comes into being when gratification, the desire for sensation, comes to an end.

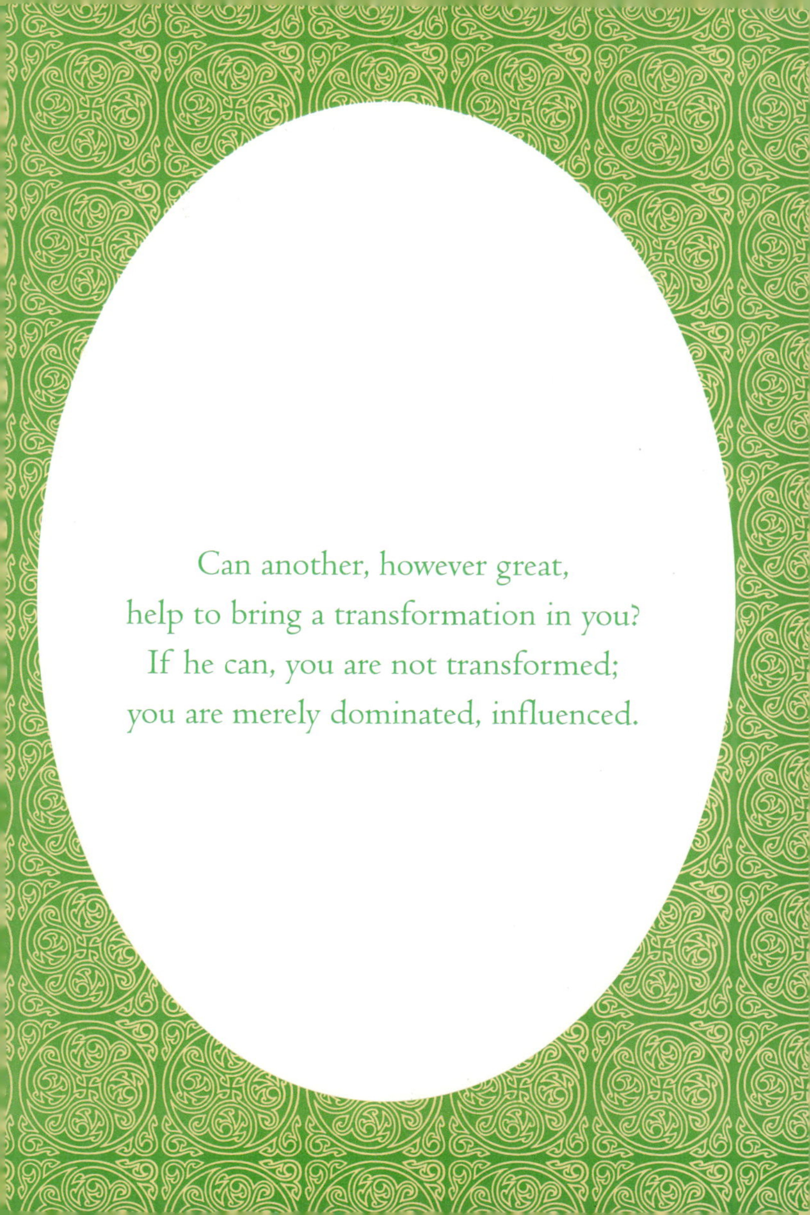

Can another, however great,
help to bring a transformation in you?
If he can, you are not transformed;
you are merely dominated, influenced.

Love is a flame without smoke.

Action towards a predetermined goal
is not action at all,
but conformity to belief, to an idea.

Meditation is freeing the mind
of its own thoughts at all levels.

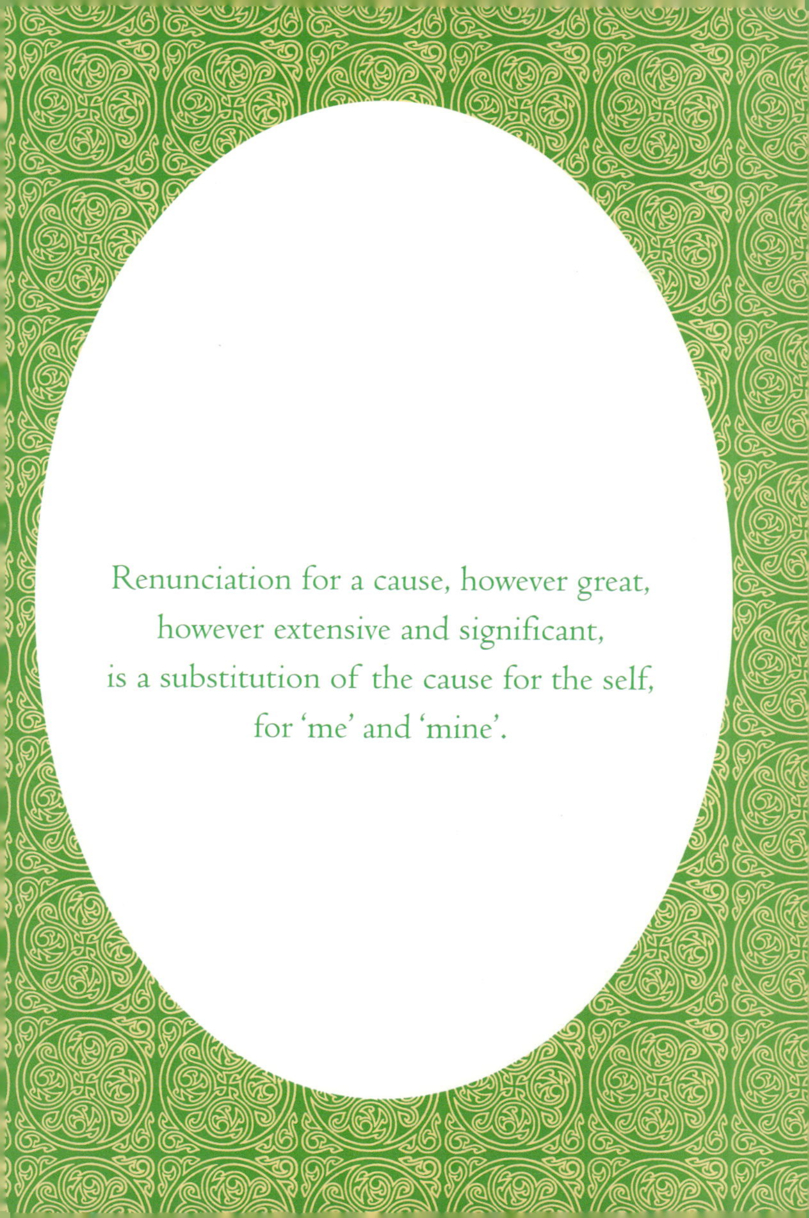

Renunciation for a cause, however great,
however extensive and significant,
is a substitution of the cause for the self,
for 'me' and 'mine'.

Merely to say that we cannot help it,
puts an end to discussion.
It is a sluggish mind that makes this suggestion
and puts up with suffering.

Love that turns to sorrow or to hate
is not love at all.

Life is more intimate among the less educated,
where the fever of ambition
has not yet spread.

To be still after tilling and sowing
is to give birth to creation.

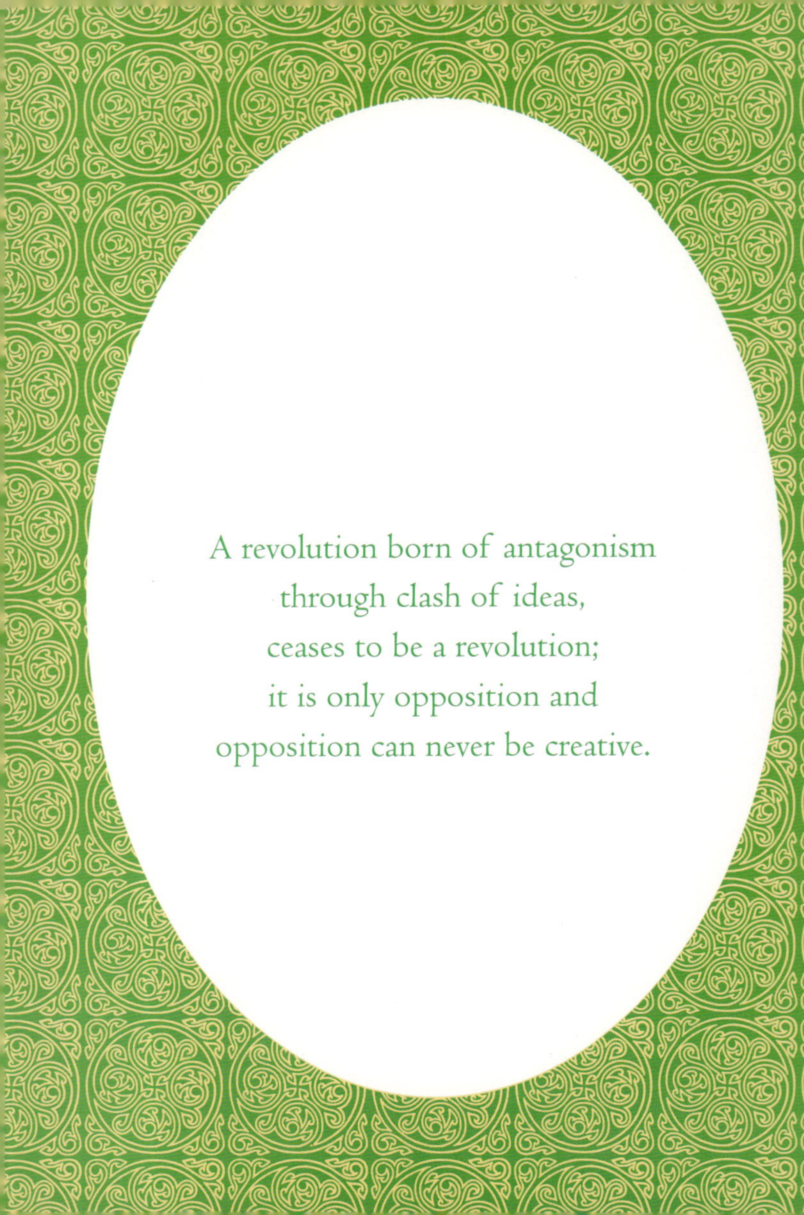

A revolution born of antagonism
through clash of ideas,
ceases to be a revolution;
it is only opposition and
opposition can never be creative.

The mind is quiet only when
it is not caught in thought.

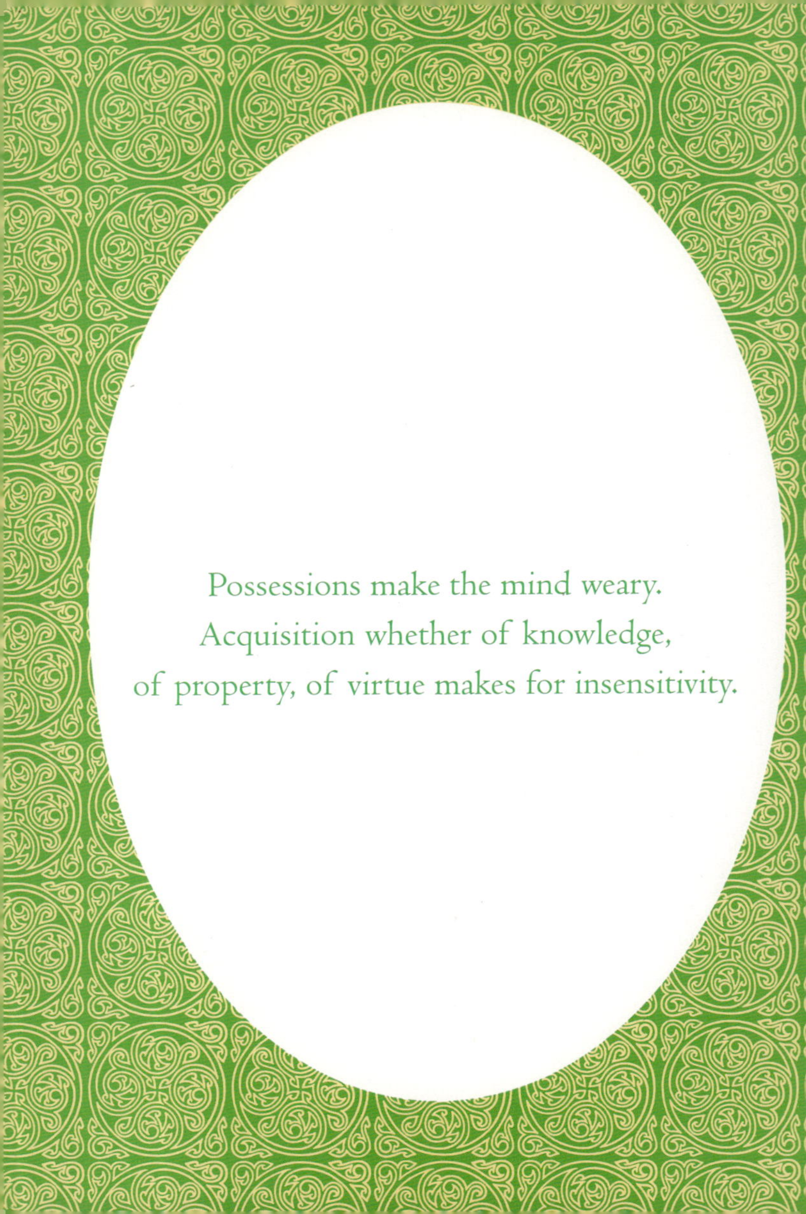

Possessions make the mind weary.
Acquisition whether of knowledge,
of property, of virtue makes for insensitivity.

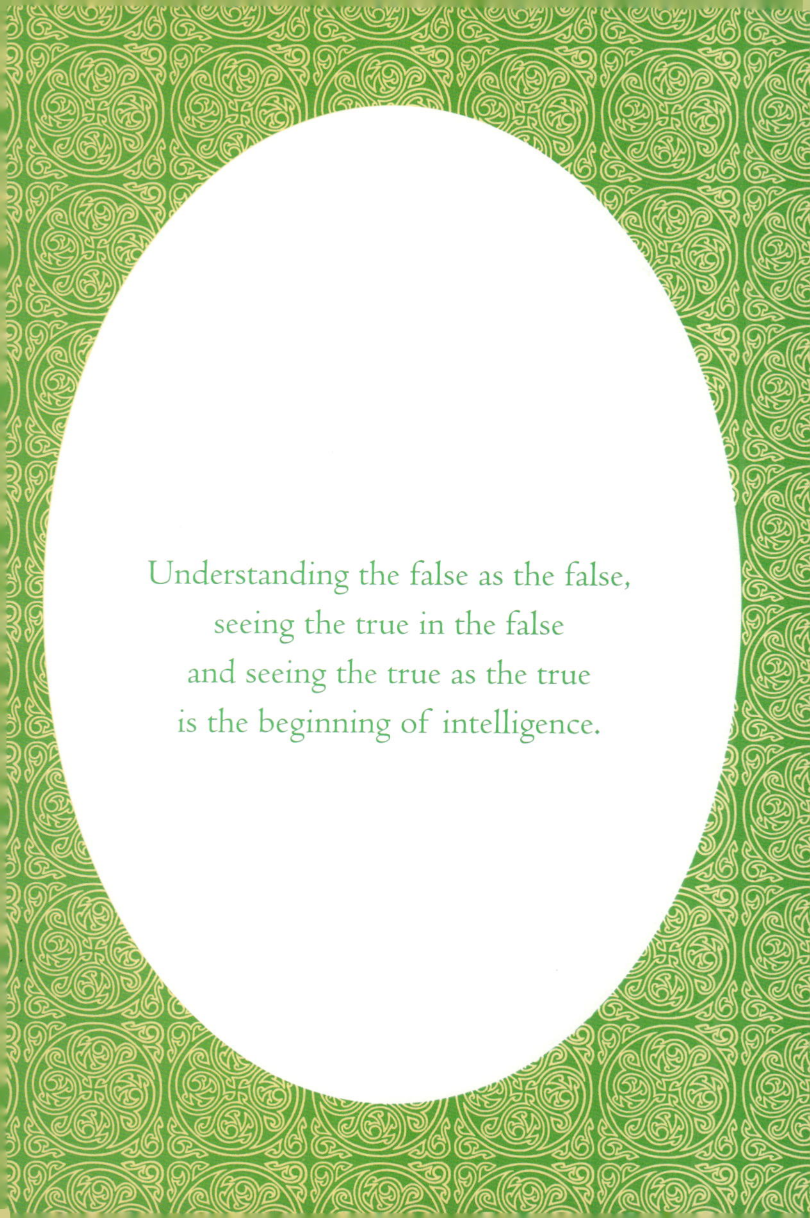
Understanding the false as the false,
seeing the true in the false
and seeing the true as the true
is the beginning of intelligence.

Chastity is not a thing of the mind;
chastity is the very nature of love.
Without love there can be no true chastity.

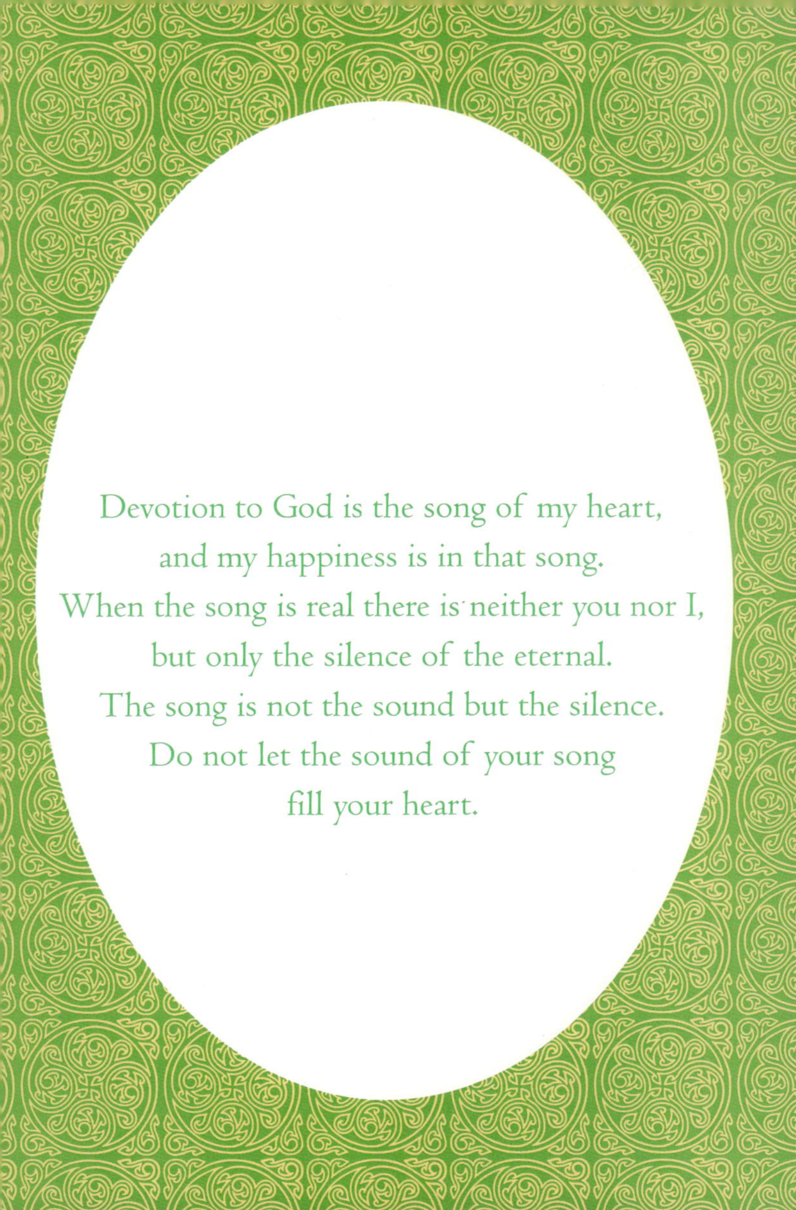

Devotion to God is the song of my heart,
and my happiness is in that song.
When the song is real there is neither you nor I,
but only the silence of the eternal.
The song is not the sound but the silence.
Do not let the sound of your song
fill your heart.

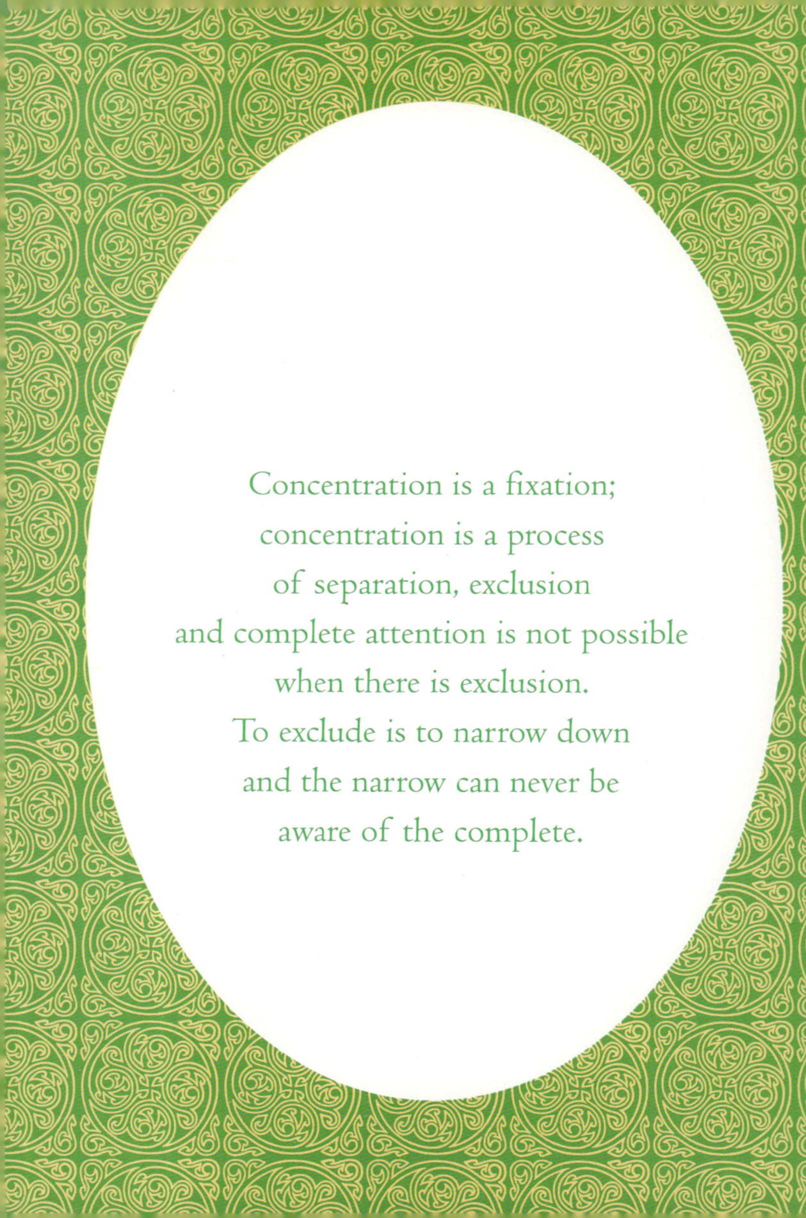

Concentration is a fixation;
concentration is a process
of separation, exclusion
and complete attention is not possible
when there is exclusion.
To exclude is to narrow down
and the narrow can never be
aware of the complete.

As long as 'the more' is a means to happiness,
the end is always dissatisfaction,
conflict and misery.

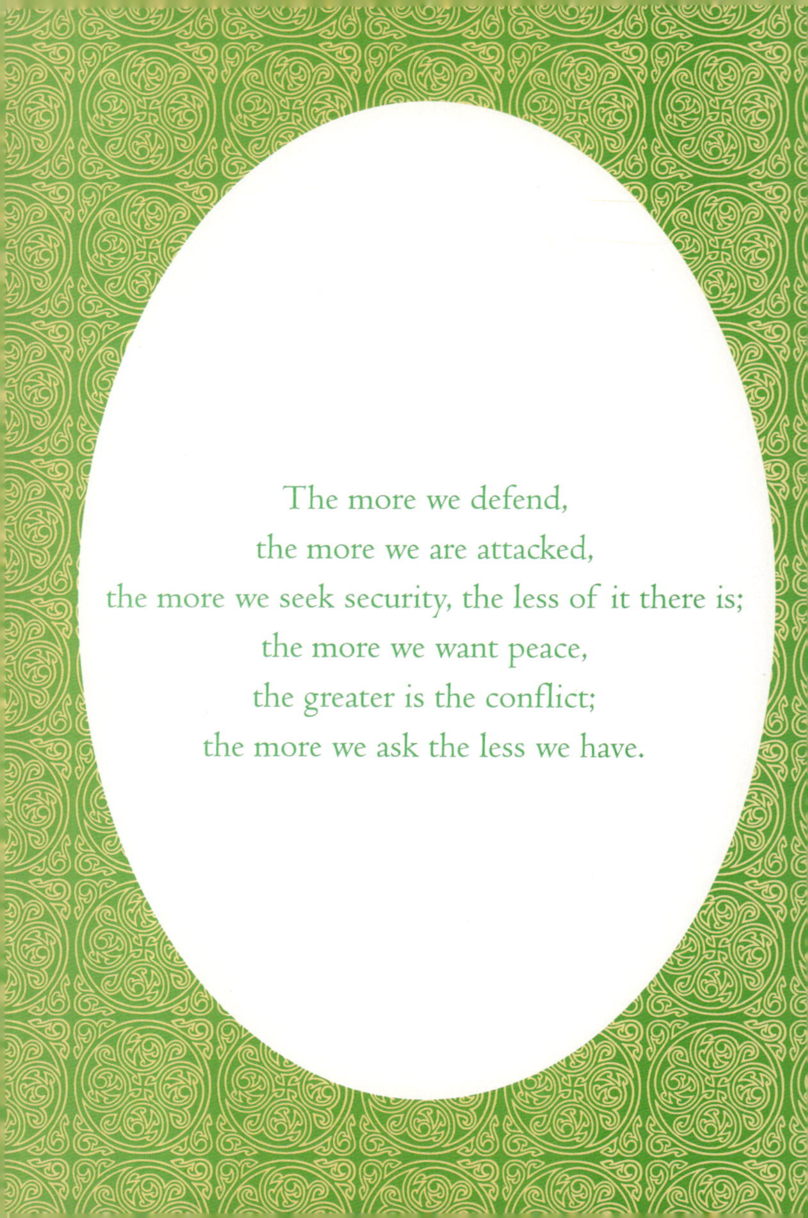

The more we defend,
the more we are attacked,
the more we seek security, the less of it there is;
the more we want peace,
the greater is the conflict;
the more we ask the less we have.

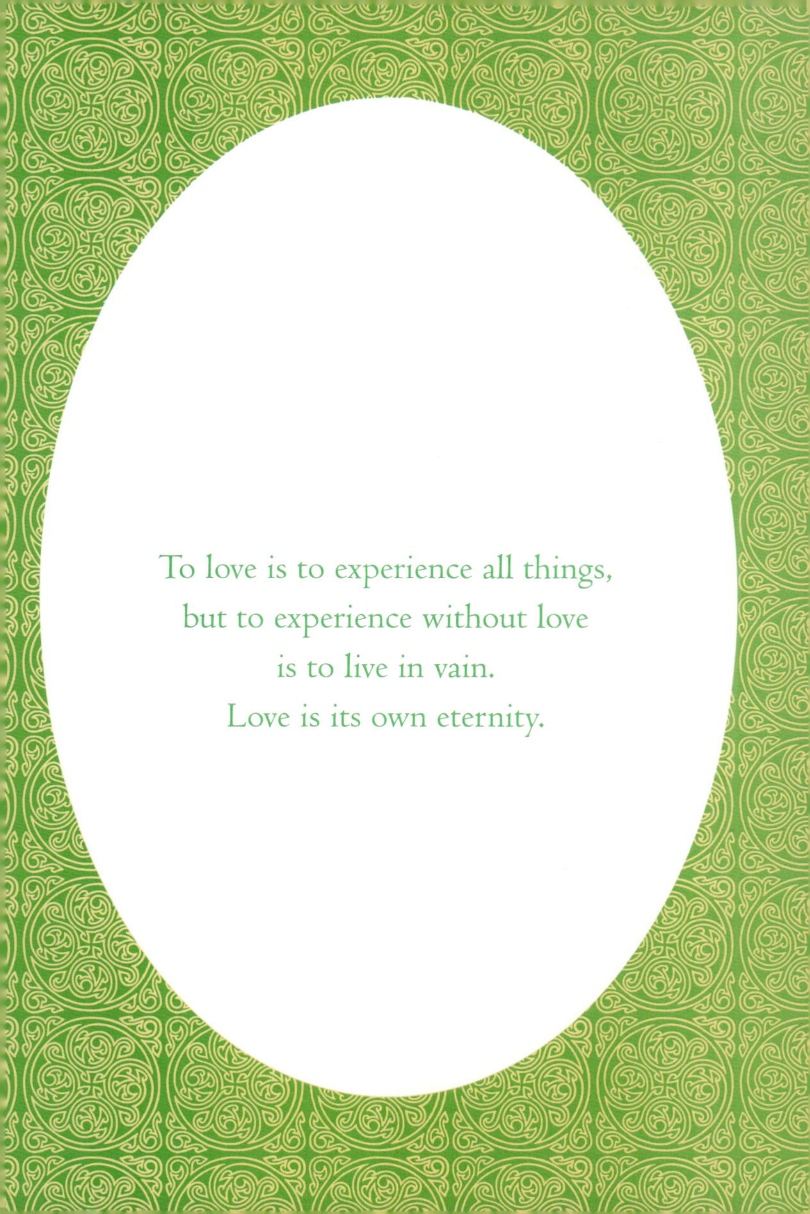

To love is to experience all things,
but to experience without love
is to live in vain.
Love is its own eternity.

A patterned society functions only within the frame of its self-projected belief.

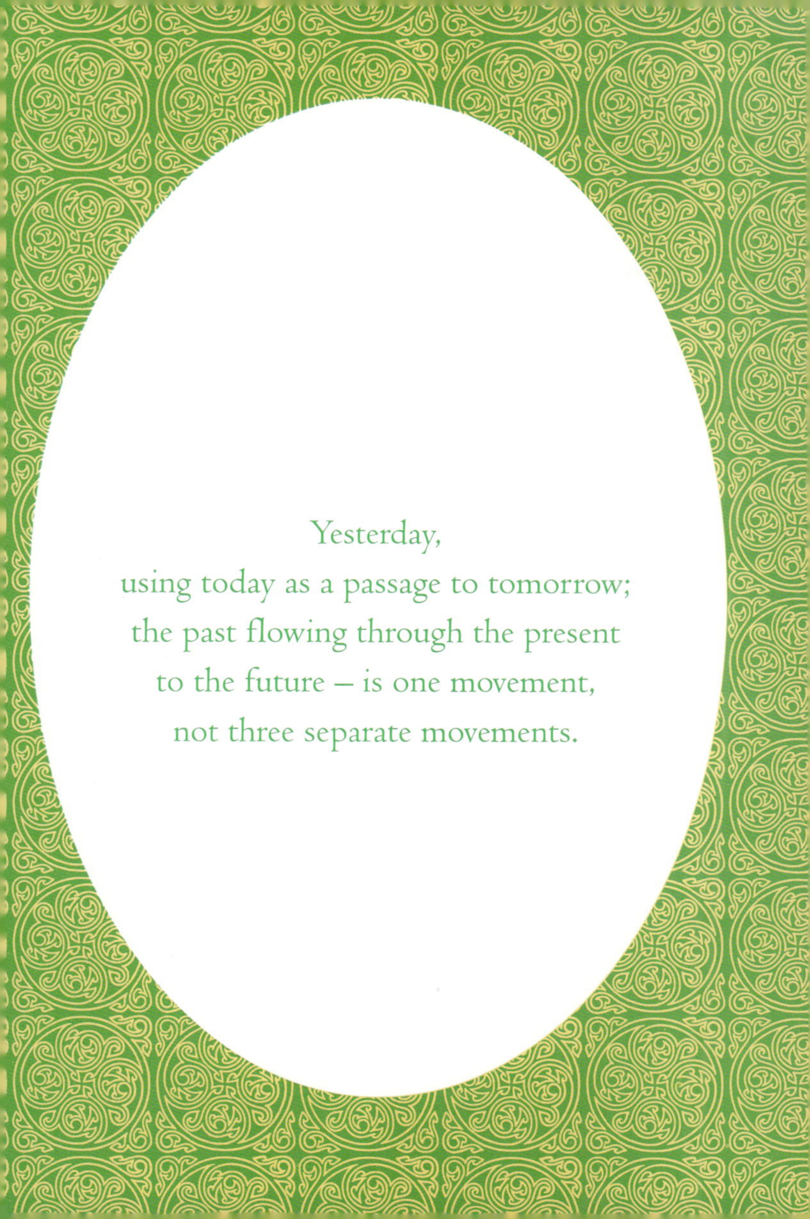

Yesterday,
using today as a passage to tomorrow;
the past flowing through the present
to the future – is one movement,
not three separate movements.

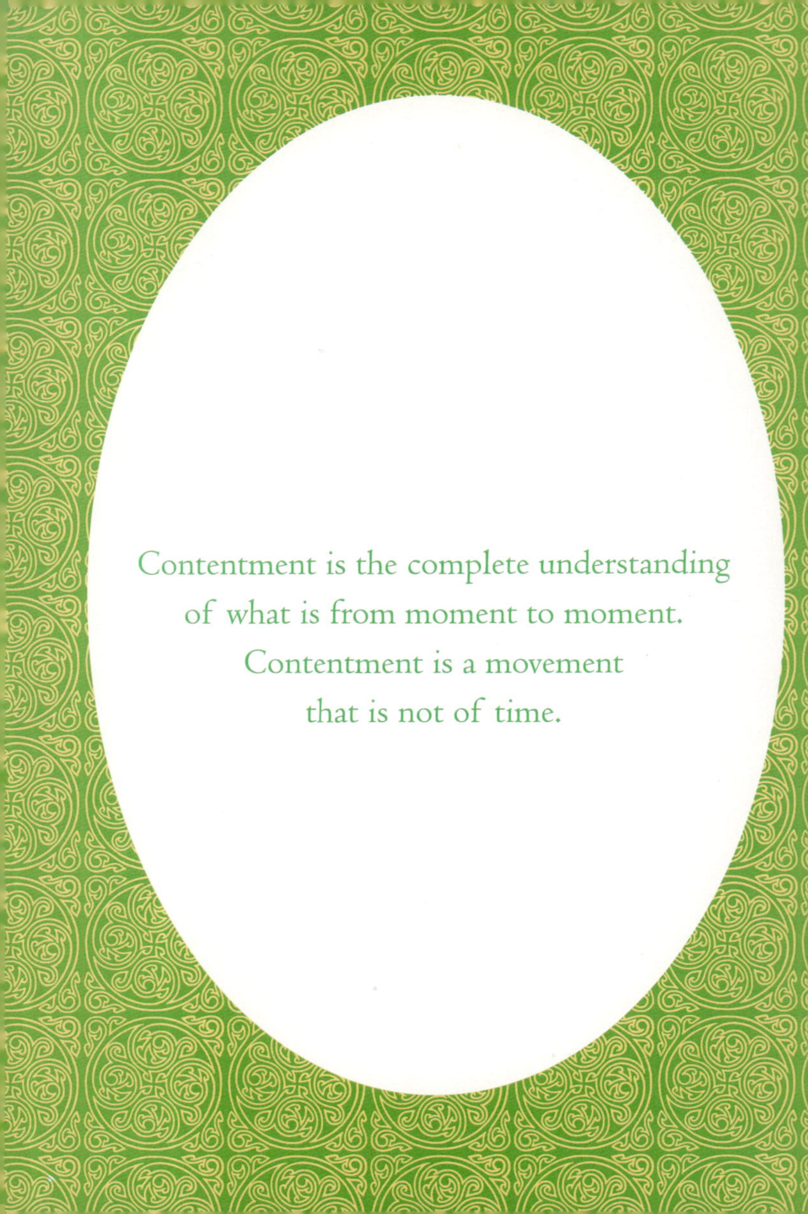
Contentment is the complete understanding
of what is from moment to moment.
Contentment is a movement
that is not of time.

Without humility, reality can never be.

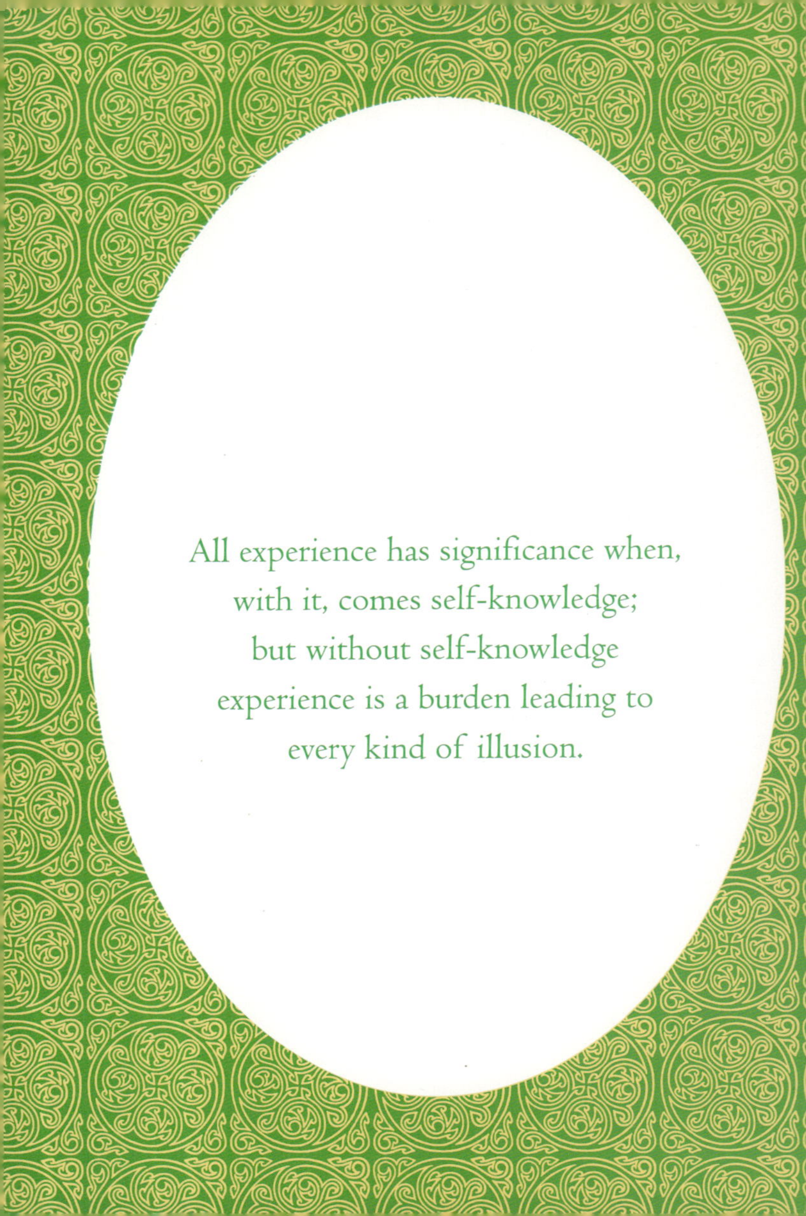

All experience has significance when, with it, comes self-knowledge; but without self-knowledge experience is a burden leading to every kind of illusion.

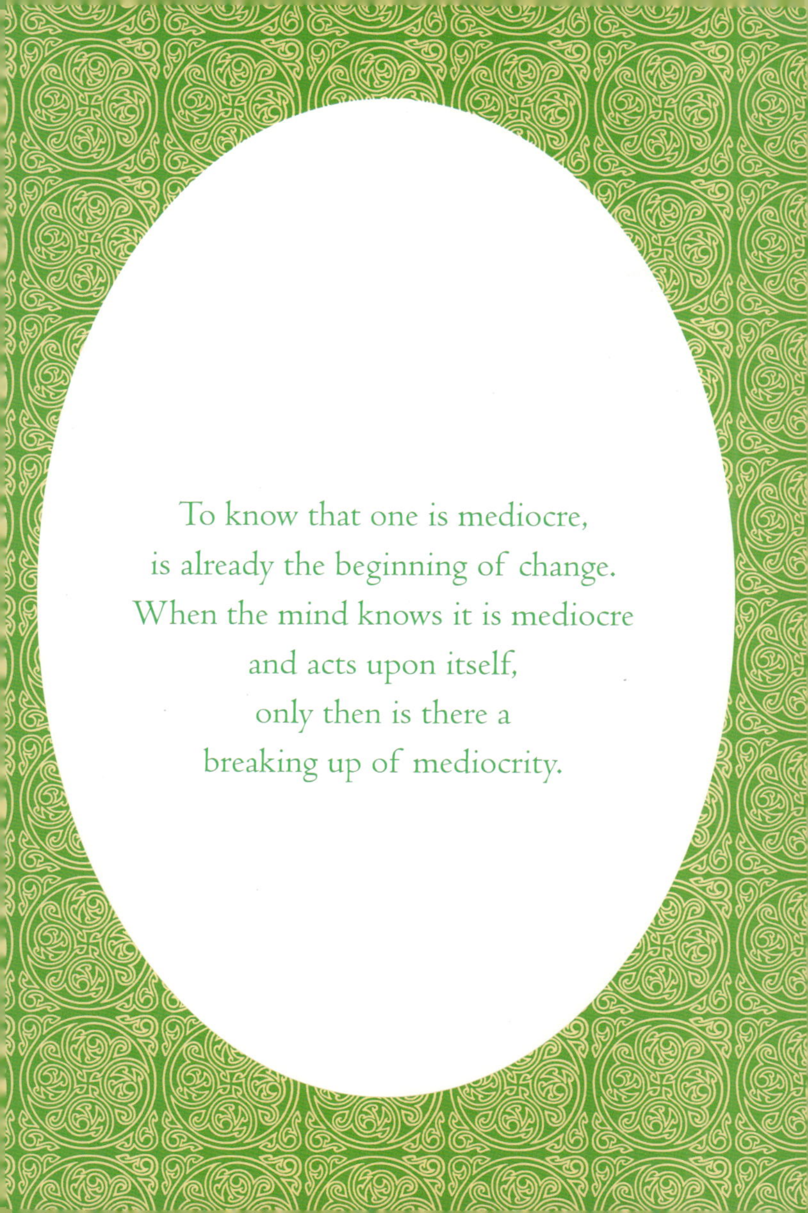

To know that one is mediocre,
is already the beginning of change.
When the mind knows it is mediocre
and acts upon itself,
only then is there a
breaking up of mediocrity.

The more you fight a habit,
the more life you give to it.
Habit is a dead thing,
do not fight it, do not resist it;
with the perception of
the truth of discontent, the past,
the habit, will loose its significance.

Imagination prevents
the perception of what is,
because it clothes itself in what should be.
The good is not in what should be,
but in understanding what is.

Reality has no continuity.
It is from moment to moment,
timeless and measureless.

Ambition breeds mediocrity of heart and mind.
The urge to be successful strengthens the ego,
whose very structure is brittle,
superficial and limited.

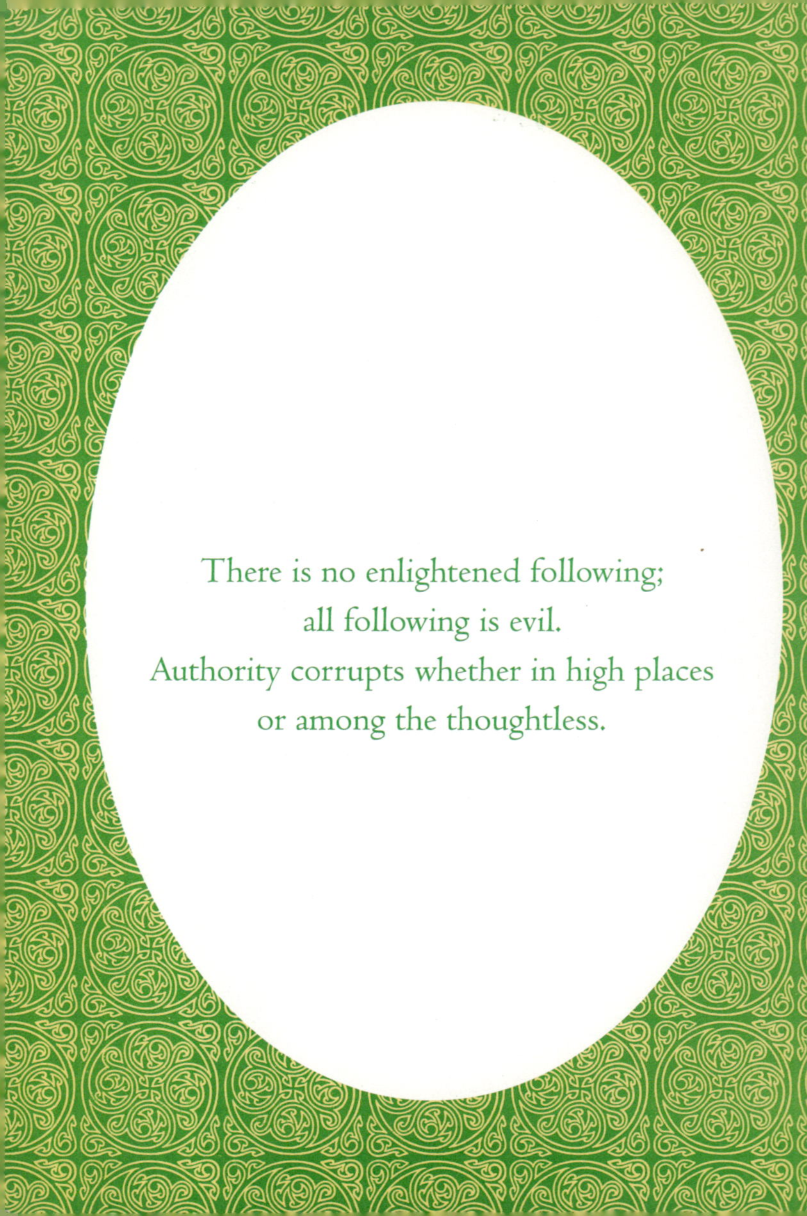

There is no enlightened following;
all following is evil.
Authority corrupts whether in high places
or among the thoughtless.

The still silence of the mind comes
when there is no seeker,
no desire for seeking.

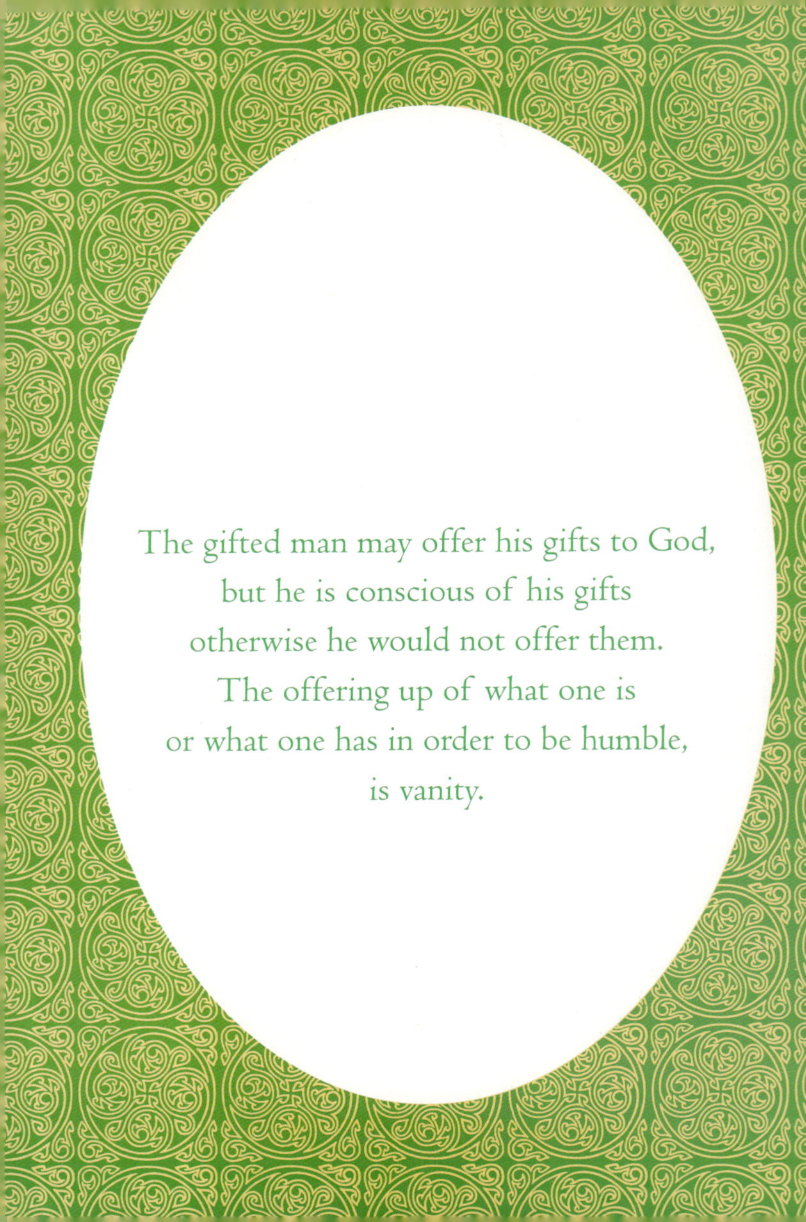

The gifted man may offer his gifts to God,
but he is conscious of his gifts
otherwise he would not offer them.
The offering up of what one is
or what one has in order to be humble,
is vanity.

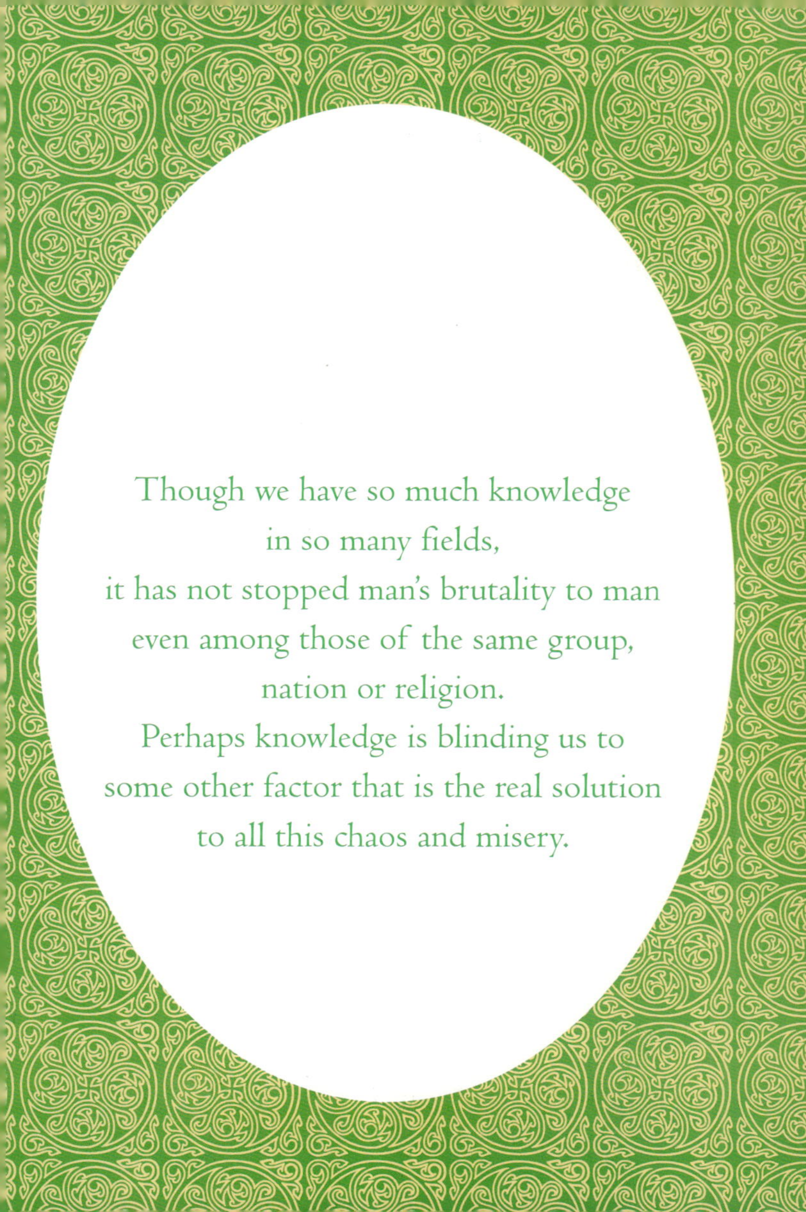

Though we have so much knowledge
in so many fields,
it has not stopped man's brutality to man
even among those of the same group,
nation or religion.
Perhaps knowledge is blinding us to
some other factor that is the real solution
to all this chaos and misery.

The perception of the false as the false
is the ending of the false.

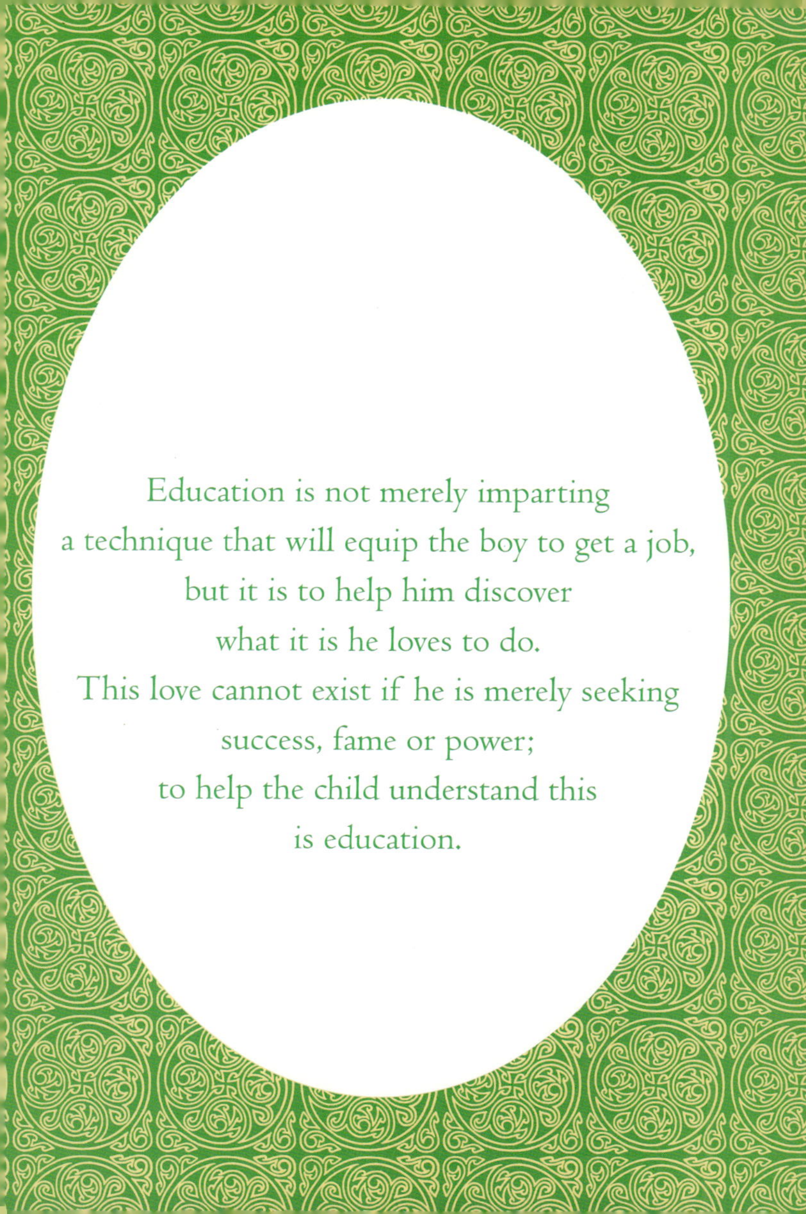

Education is not merely imparting
a technique that will equip the boy to get a job,
but it is to help him discover
what it is he loves to do.
This love cannot exist if he is merely seeking
success, fame or power;
to help the child understand this
is education.

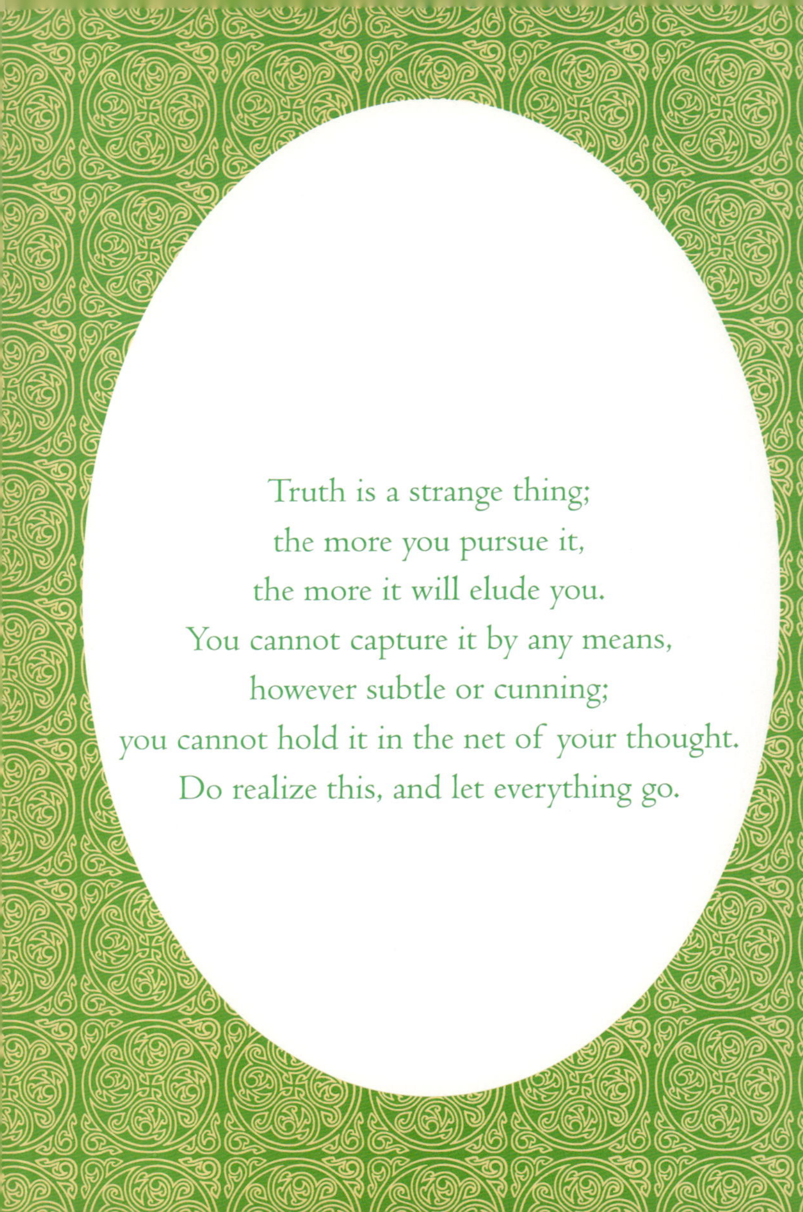

Truth is a strange thing;
the more you pursue it,
the more it will elude you.
You cannot capture it by any means,
however subtle or cunning;
you cannot hold it in the net of your thought.
Do realize this, and let everything go.

The action of love has no motive –
every other action has.

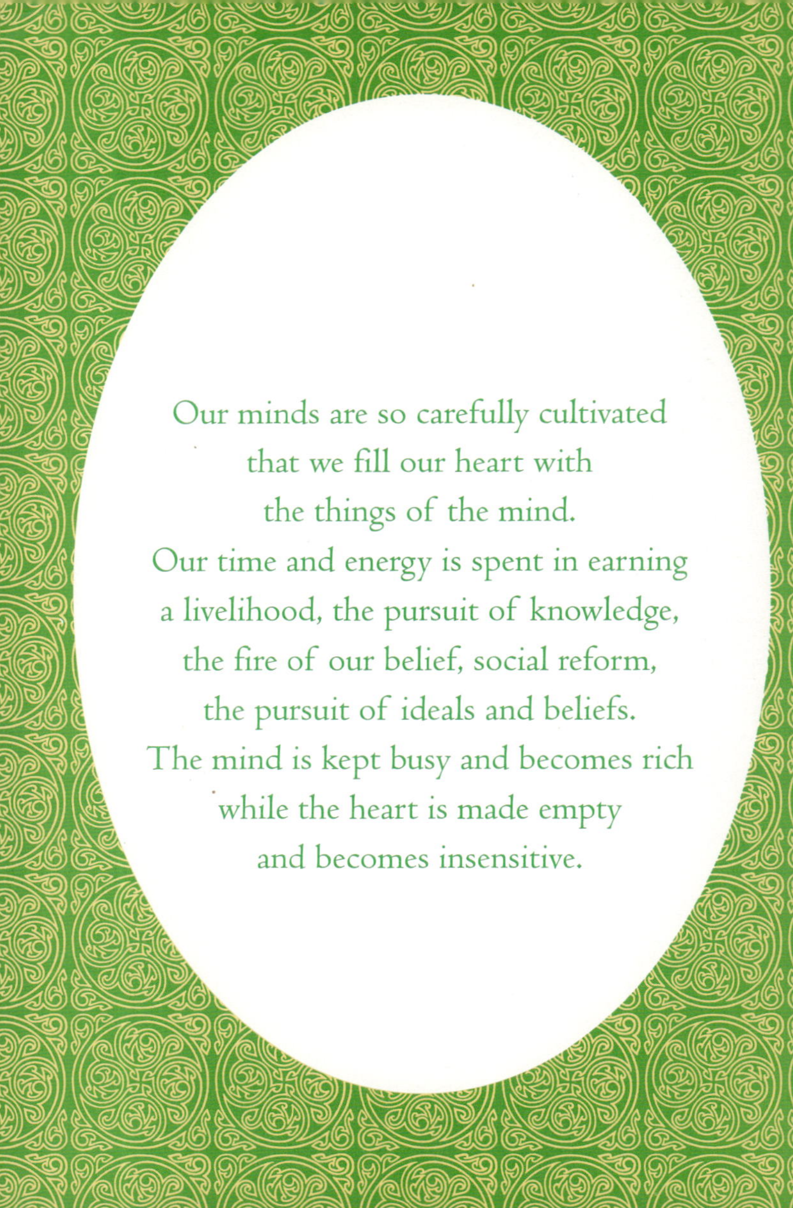

Our minds are so carefully cultivated
that we fill our heart with
the things of the mind.
Our time and energy is spent in earning
a livelihood, the pursuit of knowledge,
the fire of our belief, social reform,
the pursuit of ideals and beliefs.
The mind is kept busy and becomes rich
while the heart is made empty
and becomes insensitive.

Hate can only breed further hate;
and a society based on hate, on envy
will always be at war within itself
and with other societies.

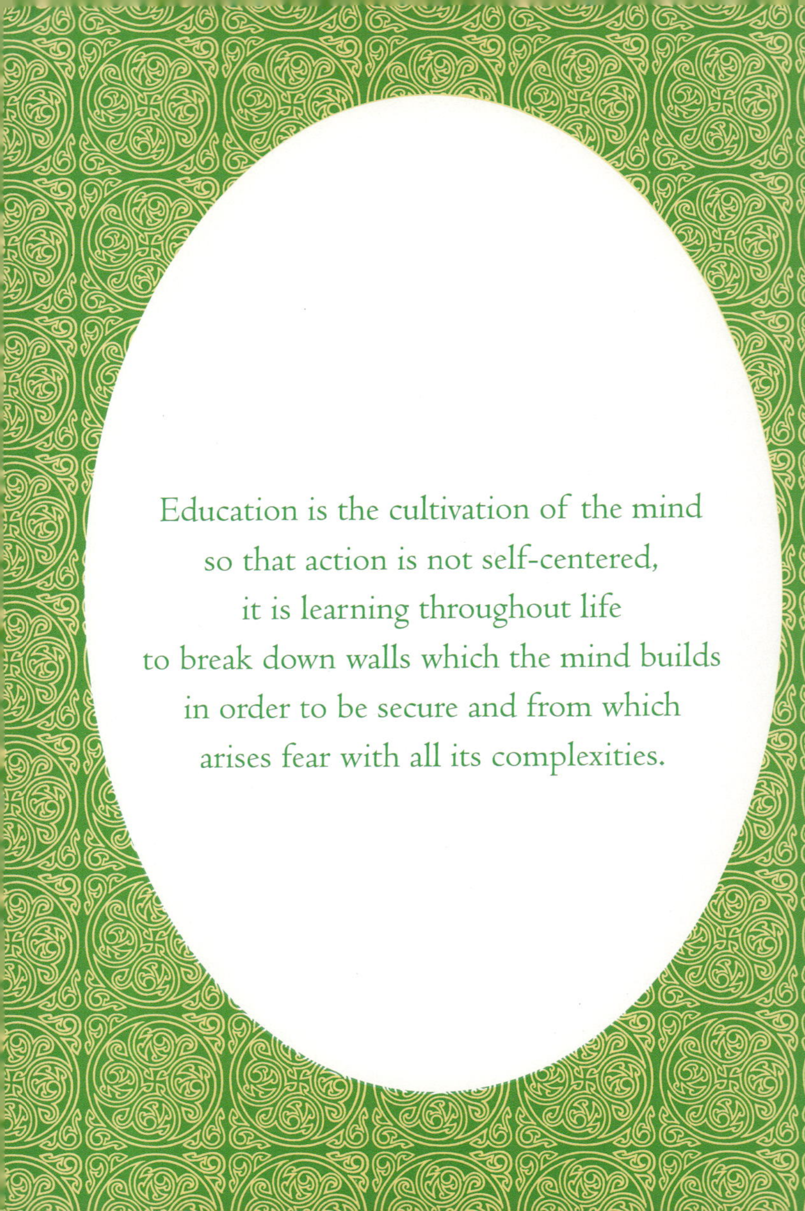

Education is the cultivation of the mind
so that action is not self-centered,
it is learning throughout life
to break down walls which the mind builds
in order to be secure and from which
arises fear with all its complexities.

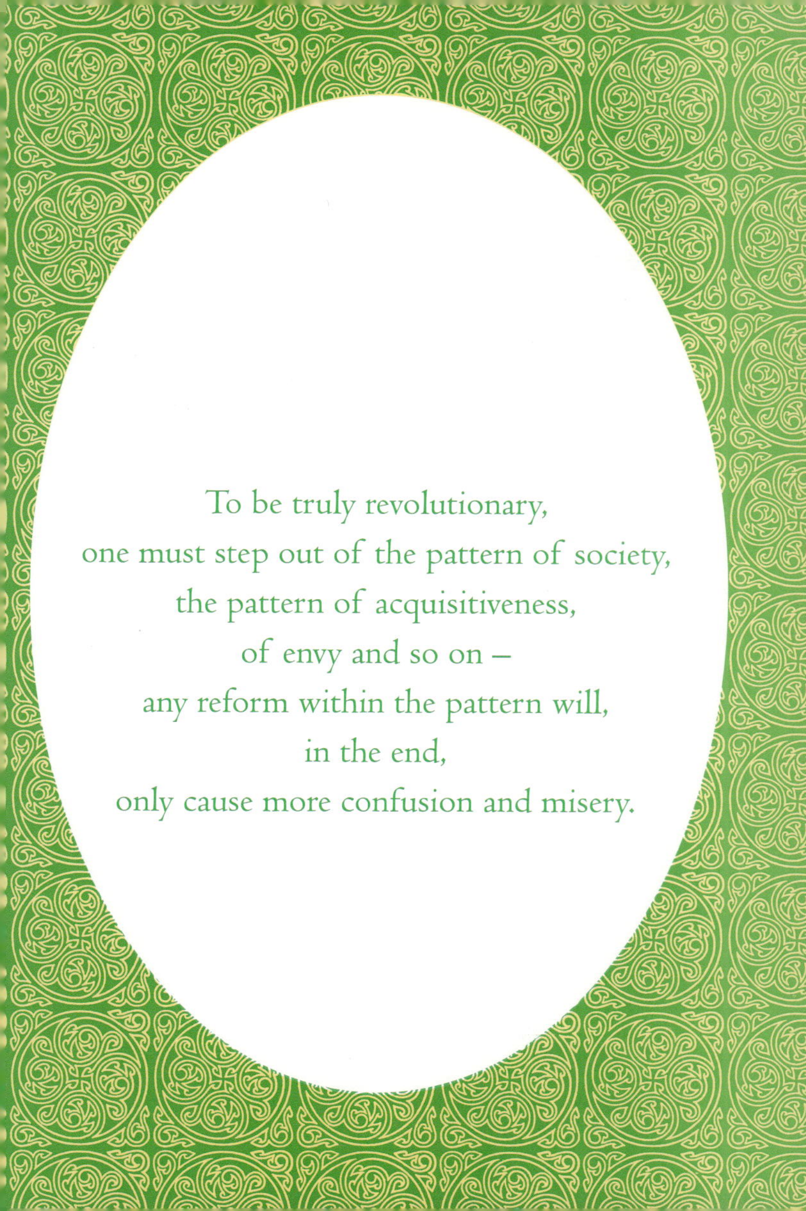

To be truly revolutionary,
one must step out of the pattern of society,
the pattern of acquisitiveness,
of envy and so on –
any reform within the pattern will,
in the end,
only cause more confusion and misery.

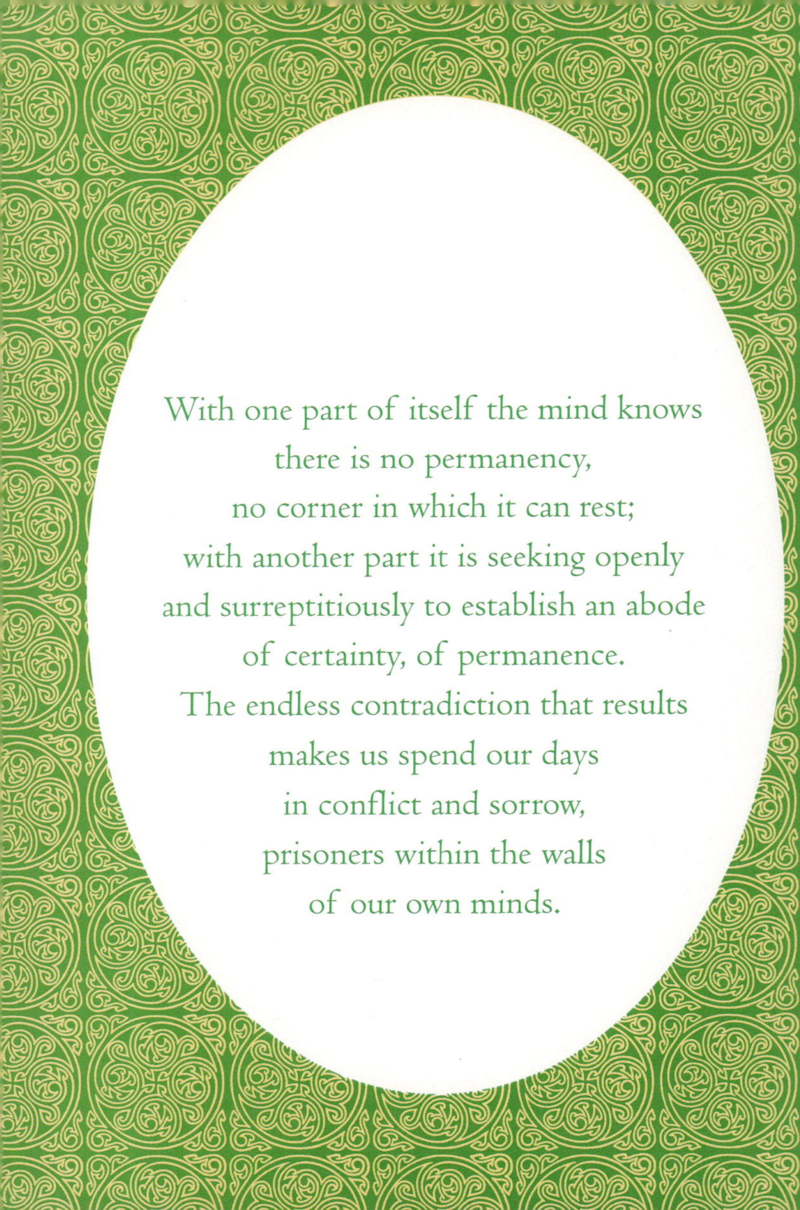

With one part of itself the mind knows
there is no permanency,
no corner in which it can rest;
with another part it is seeking openly
and surreptitiously to establish an abode
of certainty, of permanence.
The endless contradiction that results
makes us spend our days
in conflict and sorrow,
prisoners within the walls
of our own minds.

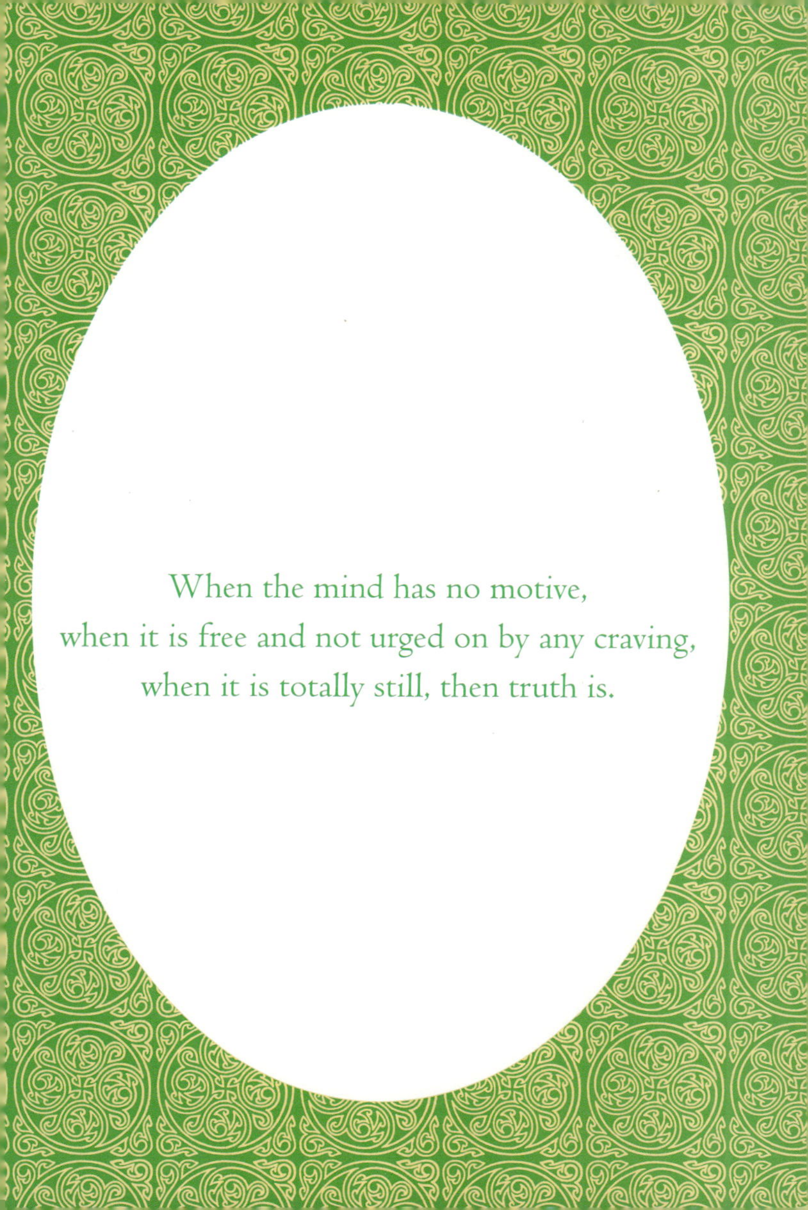

When the mind has no motive,
when it is free and not urged on by any craving,
when it is totally still, then truth is.

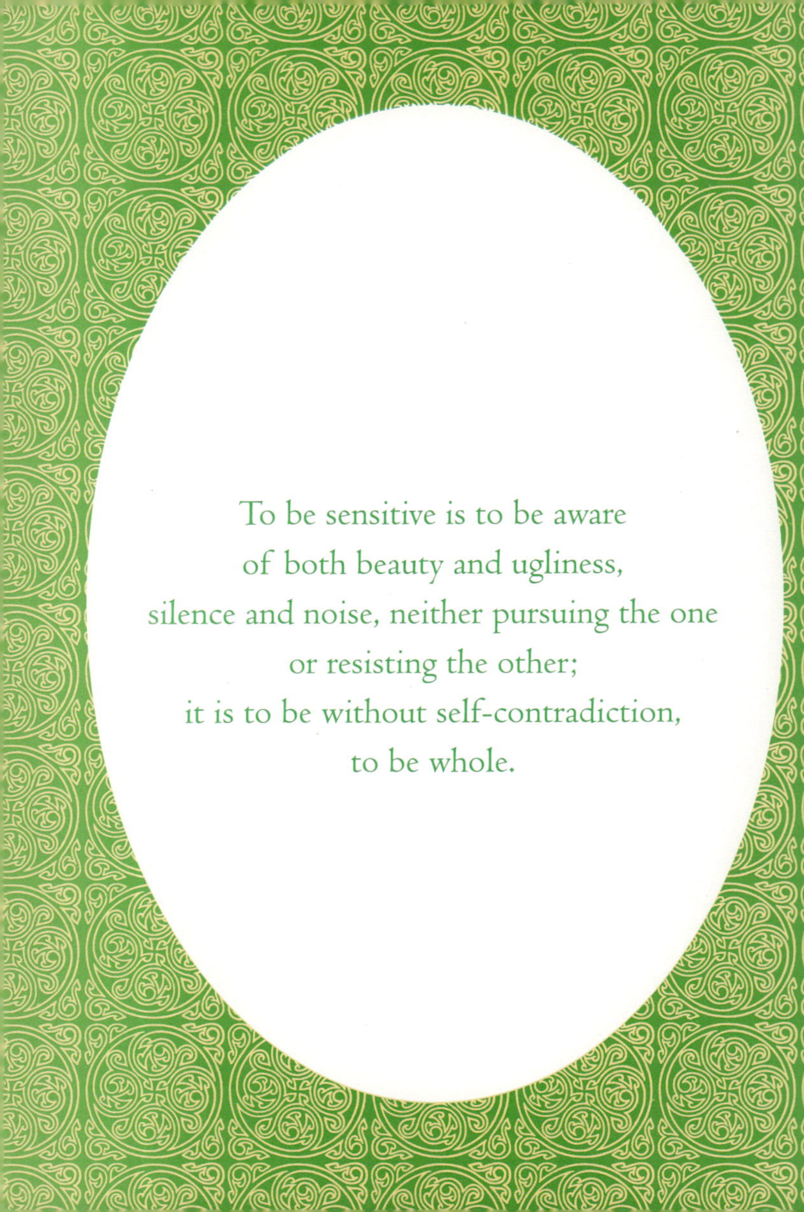

To be sensitive is to be aware
of both beauty and ugliness,
silence and noise, neither pursuing the one
or resisting the other;
it is to be without self-contradiction,
to be whole.

All compulsion, however subtle,
is the outcome of ignorance;
it is born of the desire for reward
or the fear of punishment.

Ambition to fulfill or to become something has always, within it, the seed of frustration, fear and sorrow.
This self-centered activity is in the very nature of egotism.

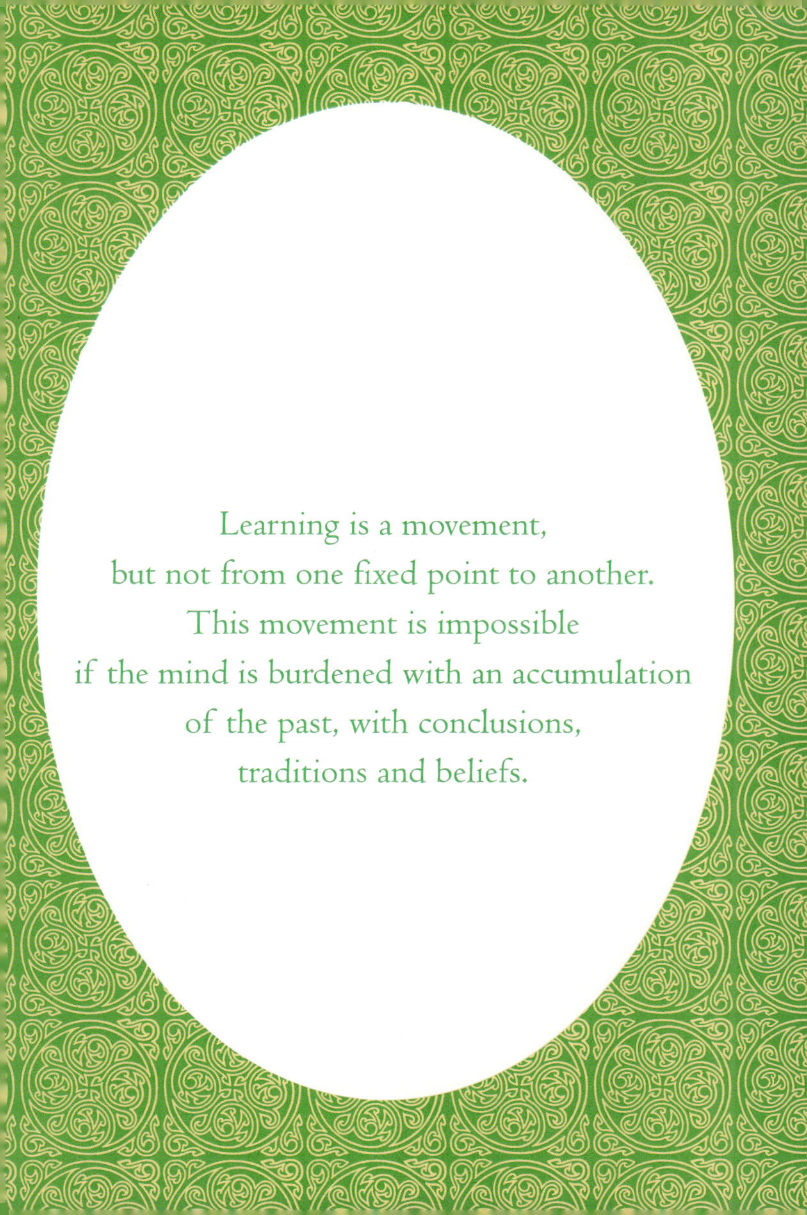

Learning is a movement,
but not from one fixed point to another.
This movement is impossible
if the mind is burdened with an accumulation
of the past, with conclusions,
traditions and beliefs.

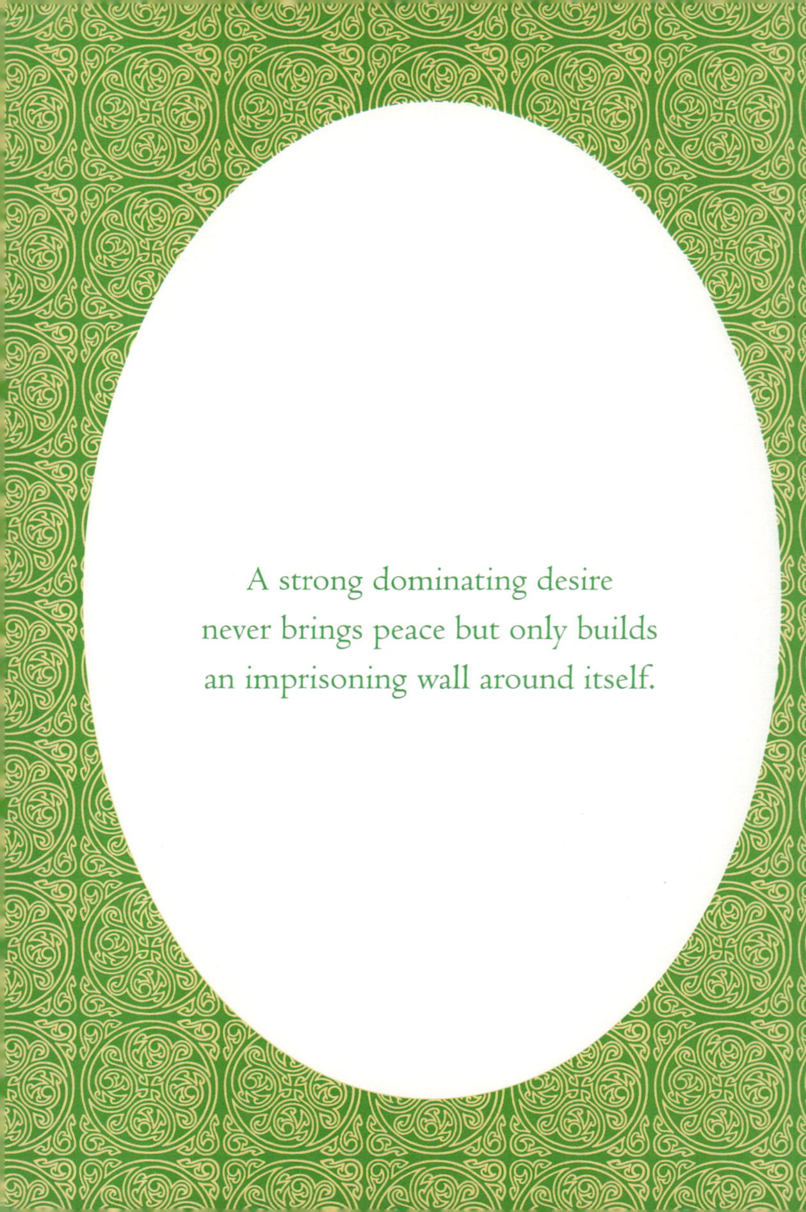
A strong dominating desire
never brings peace but only builds
an imprisoning wall around itself.

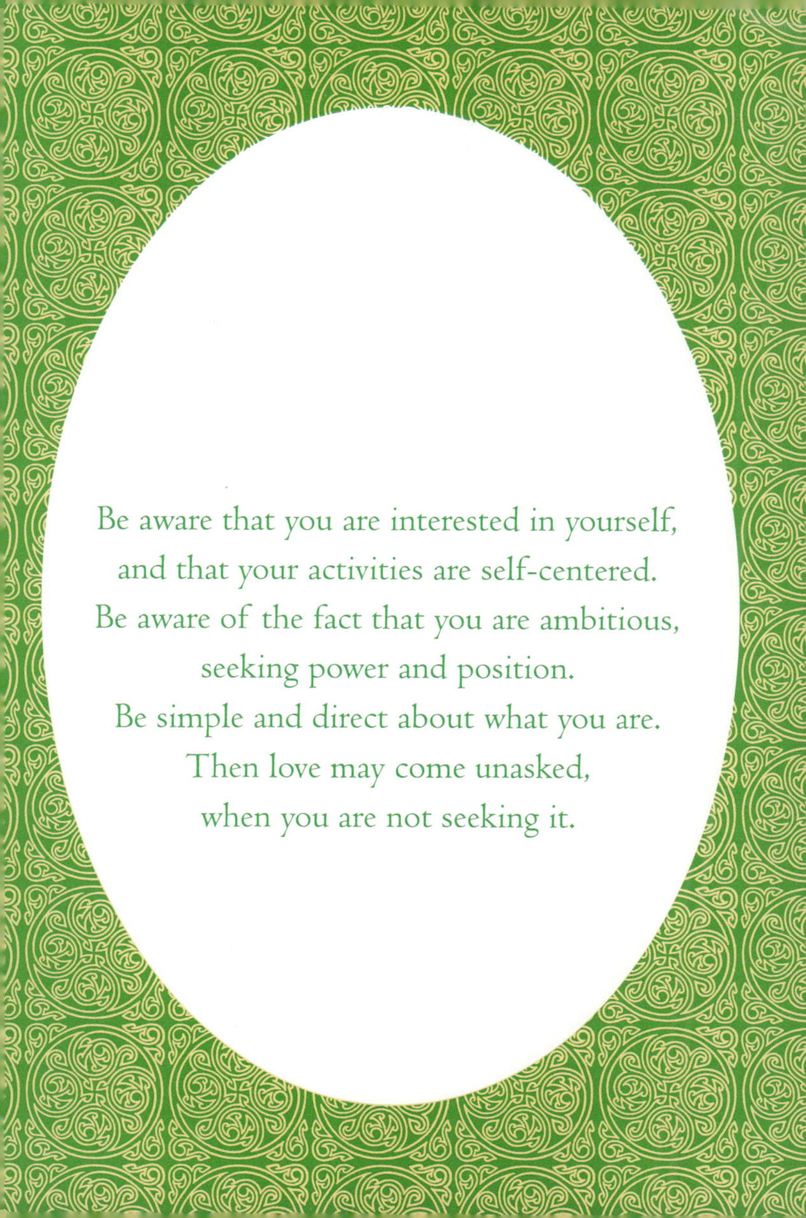

Be aware that you are interested in yourself,
and that your activities are self-centered.
Be aware of the fact that you are ambitious,
seeking power and position.
Be simple and direct about what you are.
Then love may come unasked,
when you are not seeking it.

We are the things we possess,
we are that to which we are attached.

Notes

Notes